The Shropshire Severn

Edited by Richard K Morriss

Shropshire Books

Front cover: River Severn near Wroxeter, photo Gordon Dickins
Back Cover: River Severn at Atcham, photo Gordon Dickins

© Richard K Morriss and other contributors
ISBN: 0-903802-61-9
Cover and Book design: Daywell Designs
Colour map: Judy Whittlestone
Managing Editor: Helen Sample
Published by Shropshire Books, the Publishing Division of the Leisure Services
Department of Shropshire County Council
Printed by: Precision Colour Printing Ltd., Haldane, Halesfield 1, Telford, Shropshire TF7 4QQ.

Acknowledgements

The publishers would like to thank the following contributors to this book: David Pannett for 'The Physical Background'; Dr Paul Stamper for 'The Medieval River'; Dr Barrie Trinder, Senior Research Fellow at the Ironbridge Institute, for 'The Navigation'; John Tucker for 'Flora and Fauna'; Wayne Baker of the National Rivers Authority for 'Managing the River'; Gwen Simmonds for her poem 'To Buildwas Bridge by Severnside' on p91; Judy Whittlestone for her beautiful map on pvii; Sarah Whild for her drawings on pp114, 115, Richard K Morriss for the Introduction, 'The Coracle', 'Bridges over the Shropshire Severn', 'Recreation' and all his hard work as title editor, and Sarah Barker and her descendants for their final supreme effort.

Thanks are also due to the following for their kind permission to reproduce illustrations in this book: The Science Museum for de Loutherbourg's 'Coalbrookdale by Night' p74; The Ironbridge Gorge Museum for pp80, 83, 84, 85, 133; Gordon Dickins for pp8, 10, 13, 17, 20, 30, 36, 51, 58, 61, 90, 98, 101, 110, 122, 126, 127, 128, 130; The Records and Research Department for pp4, 18, 21, 26, 32, 38, 45, 48, 55, 56, 57, 60, 64, 65, 66, 67, 69, 70, 72, 77, 78, 79, 82, 88, 99, 131; Shropshire Archaeological and Historical Society for p32; David Pannett for pp46, 49, 53, 112; Bob Kemp for p117; Michael Leach for pp118, 119, 120; the National Rivers Authority p124; Richard K Morriss for all other photographs.

The distribution map for the Flowering Rush on p115 is reproduced from 'The Shropshire Flora' published by The Shropshire Trust for Nature Conservation.

Contents

Map … vii

Introduction ~ Richard K Morriss … 1

The Coracle ~ Richard K Morriss … 45

The Physical Background ~ David Pannett … 47

The Medieval River ~ Paul Stamper … 63

The Navigation ~ Barrie Trinder … 77

Bridges over the Shropshire Severn ~ Richard K Morriss … 93

Flora and Fauna ~ John Tucker … 113

Managing the River ~ The National Rivers Authority … 123

Recreation ~ Richard K Morriss … 129

Suggested Reading … 135

INTRODUCTION

Three rivers rise within a few miles of each other high on a bleak Welsh mountain. An old Welsh song, now lost, tells of these three springs being sisters. One day they decide to go down to the sea on the following morning. The first rises early, and takes a long, gentle route through several counties, including Shropshire and Worcestershire. The second rises a little later and hurries down through Herefordshire to meet her sister near Chepstow. The third gets up so late that she has to rush down to the sea by the quickest route, towards Aberystwyth. These three became the Severn, the Wye, and the Rheidol.

Two hundred and twenty miles, more or less, in length, the River Severn is the longest in Britain. Historically it has also been one of the most important. It was always a natural boundary between the mountains of western Britain and the fertile midlands to the east. Later it became a natural boundary between kingdoms, counties, bishoprics and parishes. The valley has been a routeway for thousands of years, and the river itself an important transport artery until quite recently. All of the county towns of the four historic counties through which the Severn flows are on or near to its banks - Montgomery, Shrewsbury, Worcester and Gloucester.

For nearly seventy of the most twisting and turning miles of its journey, the Severn flows through Shropshire. This section is the most varied and, arguably, the most attractive. The river has, throughout history, had a tremendous influence on the county, on the region, and, indirectly, on the whole world.

To the Welsh, the river is the Afon Hafren. It crosses into Shropshire under the brooding shadow of the Breiddens - the last bastion of upland Wales. The Romans knew the river as Sabrina, but the English have been calling it the Severn since at least the early eighth century. There is a reference to

Melverley Church

the *Saefyrne* in 706 AD. By the time it reaches the border the river has already travelled a long way from high on the bare slopes of Plynlimon, less than fifteen miles from the coast. At first little more than a mountain brook running through the vast conifer plantations of the Hafren Forest, by Llandidloes the river is more distinct. Flowing on through Caersws and Newtown, it leaves the confines of its narrow upland valley close to Montgomery.

At first the river turns to the north, as if to head towards the sea near Chester. Then, after skirting the north-western flank of the Long Mountain, it changes its mind and turns towards the east - and Shropshire. Close to the Welsh village of Crew Green, it is joined by the Afon Vyrnwy. This too flows north before turning to the east below the quarry-scarred cliffs of Llanymynech. For much of its length, the Vyrnwy marks the border between England and Wales. For a mile or so below the confluence the Severn takes on that role before finally leaving the Principality behind.

Introduction

The first English village the river passes is Melverley. It is a pleasant and peaceful enough place in summer when water levels are low and the river flows languidly between steep-sided banks. But in the winter, especially when the rains are heavy, the runoff in the Welsh valleys causes the two rivers to rise and rage and the cry goes up 'God Help Melverley!'. This is no idle exclamation. When the floods come anxious farmers are forced to move stock from the water meadows and villagers prepare themselves for the possibility of being cut off from the rest of the world.

The churchyard is on the very edge of the Vyrnwy. Over the centuries the bank has been eroded away by the floods - giving rise to gruesome tales of coffins exposed and floating off downstream. Only recently have more sophisticated steps been taken to ensure the survival of the unique church of St. Peter's itself. It is a rare example of a timber-framed church, dating back to the sixteenth century. The interior has been compared to the inside of a timber-built man o' war - and led inevitably to stories that it is built of old ships' timbers. It most certainly is not. Indeed, almost no timber-framed buildings are or ever have been.

Past Melverley the river takes a broad and lazy sweep north towards Edgerley and then slowly, almost reluctantly, turns southwards again. It flows through pastureland where, for much of the year, inquisitive young cattle graze. There are few houses in this secret landscape of wide flat fields and big skies. Narrow twisting tall-hedged lanes link the isolated farms and scattered hamlets.

It was this remoteness that attracted the austere brethren of the Grandmontine order to a priory on the river bank north of Alberbury. This was one of only three houses the order possessed in England, and the buildings were second-hand. They had been built in the early 1220's by the local lord, Fulke Fitz Warine. Fulke was something of a rebel and a rogue, often in trouble with the Crown, and always fighting. As with many such rogues, he became the stuff of legend. One tale tells that he finally realised the error of his ways and decided to found a religious house as penance for his sins. Given initially to Augustinian canons from Lilleshall, they quickly gave it back as soon as they realised

Curious cattle, near Melverley

Alberbury Priory, painted by the Rev. Williams at the end of the eighteenth century

that the lands were unprofitable. The Grandmontines moved in to what became known as the New, or Black, Abbey – though it was only ever a priory. Over the years its colour has mysteriously changed – and it has been known as the White Abbey for centuries. Because it was owned by a French order, it was taken over by the English crown quite early on and was eventually closed in 1441. Since then it has belonged to All Souls College, Oxford, and parts of the church and St. Stephen's chapel were incorporated into the present farmhouse.

There is a sad apochryphal footnote to Fulke's story. Shortly after the priory was finished, whilst sitting in his chamber, a bright and, literally, blinding light filled the room and when it faded, Fulke's sight had gone. For the last seven years of his life this adventurer bore his darkness as a patient penitent.

Alberbury itself, a mile or so over the fields, lies on the higher ground just above the flood plain. Fulke's castle still stands, close by the main road and virtually touching the parish church. The castle

Introduction

is not open to the public, but the church is well worth a visit. Dedicated to St. Michael, and surprisingly large for such a small village, the tower is of late-thirteenth century date and once carried a spire. The rest of the church was heavily restored in the nineteenth century, and the unattractive chancel was added in 1845. More restoration work at the start of this century has spruced up the church a little too much on the outside. The inside, however, is magnificent - with box-pews in a nave covered by a magnificent timber roof five hundred years old. There are many fine memorials to the Leighton family, who have lived for centuries at nearby Loton Park. This is a large mansion dating back to the late-seventeenth century but rebuilt on several occasions. The profligate Prince Regent, later George the Fourth, stayed here once. On a walk along the road to the border, tradition records that he plucked a sprig of the first tree in Wales. This is now preserved within a low stone wall and called the Prince's Oak.

The seclusion that had attracted the Grandmontines in the thirteenth century also attracted a very different type of character more than seven centuries later. During the Second World War, it was

Near Edgerley

quickly decided that some isolated areas were needed for military purposes, including that of ammunition storage. The old and virtually defunct weed-infested track of the Shropshire & Montgomeryshire Light Railway line, between Shrewsbury and Llanymynech, finally found a use. The army took it over, lock stock and decrepit barrel, and built new marshalling yards, sidings, loops and stations. Large barracks were established at Wilcot to house several hundred soldiers, and over two hundred bomb-proof ammunition depots were built, each with its own siding. Civilians were not encouraged to linger as the camouflaged ammunition trains trundled through the night. Still used after the end of the war, the army finally relinquished control in 1960 and the rails were lifted. The ammunition dumps proved harder to get rid of - and are still there. Even the most ingenious of farmers has difficulty in finding new uses for all of these free buildings. There is only so much demand for barns, cowsheds, stores and workshops. They squat ominously in the flat countryside, their harsh lines gradually being softened by creeping vegetation. The Army still use some of the land for training.

A peaceful scene near Shrawardine

Introduction

The old railway crossed the Severn near the village of Shrawardine, although the bridge has long gone. Here the river enters a more rolling and more wooded landscape and the village is on high ground overlooking a long sweep of the river. The views westwards up the valley from these parts, with the blue blur of the Welsh hills framing the horizon, are most attractive. Shrawardine - pronounced 'Shraden' - boasts the fragmentary remains of its medieval castle. This had been rebuilt by the fitzAlan family in the early thirteenth century and renamed Castle Isabel. It was taken by Parliamentary troops after a short seige in 1645, and afterwards its materials were used to reinforce the defences of Shrewsbury. The even more fragmentary earthworks of an earlier castle lie on the opposite bank, in Little Shrawardine. This was a Norman 'motte-and-bailey' built to guard what was then an important ford across the river. There were no other good crossings for many miles upstream.

In the Middle Ages the Severn between the fords at Rhydwhyman, near Montgomery, and Shrawardine marked the boundary between the diocese of Hereford and St. Asaph. After a rather bitter ecclesiastical dispute between the respective bishops in the 1280's - during which bodies were even snatched from Alberbury's graveyard - the Bishop of Hereford rode along the newly confirmed boundary one late November day granting indulgences and confirming children. Some of Shrawardine's handful of timber-framed buildings may be older than its little sandstone church. This is one of those rare churches built during the unhappy years of the Commonwealth - the nave being put up in 1649 after the village was damaged during the Civil War. The chancel was rebuilt in 1722.

A mile or so downstream of Shrawardine, the river passes between the villages of Montford, on the north bank, and Ford, on the south. Ford has a small but pretty thirteenth century church, heavily restored in 1875, and two surprisingly large Georgian houses in its old core. Montford is smaller, with a church dedicated to St. Chad's and built as recently as 1737. Thousands of children know this area well, because of the Preston Montford Field Centre used by schools all over the country.

The main road, for centuries, between Shrewsbury and North Wales has crossed the Severn by Montford Bridge, a mile or so down river from the original village. It may just be possible that this bridge crossing replaced the ford at Shrawardine early in the medieval period. Until the mid-nineteenth century Montford Bridge was the first English bridge across the Severn, and until the Melverley bridge was converted to road traffic in 1960, was still the first road bridge. One of the

The Shropshire Severn

The river at Pentre

Introduction

many tales told of Wild Humphrey Kynaston, Shropshire's answer to Robin Hood, concerns the bridge here. Kynaston lived in a cave, still in existence, on Nesscliffe, a few miles to the north. The sheriff thought he had Kynaston trapped on the Shrewsbury side of the river and had the timbers removed between one of the bridge spans. Undeterred, Kynaston spurred on his faithful steed - Beelzebub - and the two lept the yawing chasm with ease. Unlike that stone and timber bridge, the present bridge is a splendid example of stone craftmanship. It was built by Telford, and one of his toll-gate houses still stands by the main road. The new A5 by-pass now crosses by a graceless modern bridge upstream of the old, at least giving the inhabitants of the village a little peace from the incessant roar of traffic.

Battlefield church was built on the orders of Henry IV to help the souls of those killed at the Battle of Shrewsbury

From Montford Bridge to the middle of Shrewsbury is just four miles by road. The river takes well over three times that long as it flows in a series of serpentine loops. Augmented by the River Perry, which drains much of the flatter lands of the north of the county, it passes the attractive little village of Fitz. Shortly afterwards, the river embarks on its most audacious meander. The neck of this curious mushroom shaped diversion is just 300 metres wide; the river flows for nearly six miles around the aptly named Isle. The inside of the loop, with its rich farmland and shrinking lake, is virtually unknown to most Salopians. Around the outer edges, the steep banks are clothed with mixed woodlands, especially around Leaton. This is a scattered village with a distinctive Victorian church and matching former rectory by the Shrewsbury-Baschurch road. There is commercial forestry here, but some of the trees are a little more exotic than the regimented conifer. Within these woods was, until the 1950's, one of the finer mansions in the area, Leaton Knolls. Only some outbuildings, including the former walled kitchen garden, remain.

After finishing its perambulation around The Isle, the river continues on its journey. It passes the hamlet of Rossall on the south bank, and the hamlet of Berwick on the other. Before the Battle of Shrewsbury in 1403, immortalised in Shakespeare's Henry IV, the rebel forces spent the night here. According to legend, on the way to meet the king's forces, the rebel's leading light, Harry 'Hotspur' Percy of Northumberland, remembered, too late, that he had left his sword back in the village. He asked what it was called - and on being told it was Berwick, blanched. Years before it had been predicted that he would die near Berwick. He had naturally assumed that the Berwick in question would be the one on the Tweed, around which he fought so many battles with the Scots. History

The Severn at Coton Hill, Shrewsbury

Introduction

shows us he was badly mistaken, and Hotspur was killed in one of the bloodiest battles ever held on English soil - a site now marked by Battlefield church just north of Shrewsbury.

If there is a focus to Berwick, it is Berwick House and the nearby chapel and almshouses, all set in attractive parkland overlooking the river. The original character of the house of 1731 is preserved in the south-eastern front. It may have been built for a branch of the Powys family by Francis Smith of Warwick. Unfortunately, in the last century it was 'modernised' in the Victorian version of the Italianate. The once-splendid gardens laid out at the same time are slowly being restored. Nearby the tiny chapel was built in 1672. The pleasant Almshouses are of the same date - an early example of brick building laid out around a peaceful quadrangle. Down by the river, a ruined boathouse is a reminder of more leisurely times.

The river now approaches Shrewsbury but is rebuffed by the steep wooded cliffs of Shelton Rough. It turns away, recovers itself, and then tries again, more successfully, at Coton Hill. This picturesque stretch of the river, with the towering woodlands on the south bank and the peaceful meadows on the north, is not as well known as it should be. If it was, it would no doubt be safe from the traffic planners who want to ruin this peaceful northern fringe of Shrewsbury by cutting through a north-west relief road from Shelton to Harlescott. So far, only government cut-backs have stopped this desecration. It would not only damage a very attractive part of the riverscape, but also blight the residential areas along the proposed route.

Shrewsbury is a town that should need little or no introduction. A. E. Housman's, in his Shropshire Lad, is as good as anyone's: -

> High the vanes of Shrewsbury gleam
> Islanded in Severn stream;
> The bridges from the steepled crest
> Cross the water east and west.
>
> The flag of morn in conqueror's state
> Enters at the English gate;
> The vanquished eve, as night prevails,
> Bleeds upon the road to Wales.

The town, of course, is not on an island, but the loop of the Severn that almost surrounds it has acted as a moat for over a thousand years. It has protected it in turn from the English, the Viking, and the Welsh. Unlike the many other loops on the river, this particular one goes around relatively high ground, leaving room to build a town above the flood plain and one that could be defended even if the river was crossed. Now the loop protects the town against the onslaught of the motor car, though it is a losing battle.

Shrewsbury - no one really cares if it is pronounced 'Shrozebury' or 'Shroowsbury' - is the traditional site of Pengwern, the lost capital of the lost principality of Powys. The truth or otherwise of the site of Pengwern in the years after the Romans left has yet to be sorted out. It is clear that by the end of the ninth century, Shrewsbury was a thriving regional centre. By the time of the Norman Conquest it was probably one of the largest towns in Saxon England - even with a population of around two thousand people. The town prospered for most of the medieval period thanks to the wool trade and the navigable river. After a period of relative decay, the town thrived again towards the end of the 16th century - a period that has left behind some of the finest timber-framed building in the region. Held for the Crown in the Civil War, in 1645 it was one of the last towns to fall to the Parliament.

In the Georgian period Shrewsbury was a regional centre with its own fashionable 'season' - and many of the elegant brick houses built by the local gentry have survived. Shrewsbury is still an important regional centre today, and has been the county town since Shropshire was formed in Saxon times. No longer the largest town in the county - that distinction is Telford's - it is still its traditional focal point.

It has yet to become a major tourist centre, despite being one of the finest historic towns in England, and being set amidst some the country's most unspoilt and picturesque countryside. In some ways, this helps the town to retain its own individual character, a character damaged but not destroyed during wholesale redevelopments in the late 1960's and early 1970's. Many historic buildings were sacrificed then on the altar of architectural mediocrity.

Thankfully, many other buildings survived - and the list of those worth seeing is very long indeed. These include the Norman castle plugging the defensive gap in the neck of the river loop and rebuilt by Edward the First; the Abbey, often ignored because it is outside the loop; several other fine churches, from medieval St. Mary's to the remarkable round-naved late-eighteenth

This tranquil rural scene is in the very heart of Shrewsbury, taken from Port Hill bridge

century St. Chad's; the sixteenth century Market Hall in the Square; the Library in Castlegates, once home to Shrewsbury School; the former Royal Shrewsbury Infirmary; the now-threatened fiery bricked late-Victorian Eye, Ear & Throat Hospital on Town Walls; and, no doubt missed by virtually all visitors, the late eighteenth century former flax mill at Ditherington - the first iron-framed building in the world.

The town's streets are lined with buildings constructed in a variety of materials, from elaborate timber-framing to rich red brick and crisp Grinshill stone. Many that appear to be brick are in fact much older than they seem and were just modernised by their owners once timber-framing had ceased to be fashionable. Set-piece streetscapes include the long rising curve of the Wyle Cop, topped by the Lion Hotel; the medieval timber-framed ranges of Butcher Row, including, in the Abbots House, original shop windows dating back to about 1460; the aptly named Grope Lane, where the buildings overhang so much in their upper stories they almost touch; and the Georgian elegance of St. John's Street, incongruously but perfectly finished off as a view by the brick tower of the otherwise bland 1960's Market complex.

Shrewsbury, refreshingly, seems to be a town that enjoys its river. It is the backdrop to so many of the town's annual events and to its daily life. Two of the largest attractions in the region's calendar are both held close to it - the ever-popular West Mid Show on its own showground, and the world-renowned Shrewsbury Flower Show in the Quarry Park. In summer, cricket is played on the tree-fringed Frankwell meadows, and competitive rowing regattas are held on the river below the loftily sited Shrewsbury School - one of the most respected of public schools. Most locals indulge in less strenuous activities - a gentle strolls along the river bank, or perhaps a lazy row on the water, or a drink in one of the beer gardens that slope down to the water's edge. Even culture comes to the river - the new arts centre, the Gateway in Chester Street, has been built overlooking it. Given all this, perhaps only a town like Shrewsbury could have a railway station with its platforms across the river, a floating Thai restaurant, and a football club with its Gay Meadow ground on the river bank in the heart of the town; kicking the ball over the stand at Shrewsbury Town FC is an expensive business.

In the stretch of river between the Welsh and English bridges, the town can boast one of the best examples of urban riverscape in England. On one side is the Quarry itself, with vast expanse of close-cropped sloping lawn, avenues of mature lime trees, and the delightful floral Dingle hidden

Shrewsbury's famous daffodils frame this view of the English Bridge

away in the middle. On the other bank, contented cows graze in Beck's Field, occasionally paddling in the cool water. They are unaware that they are standing close to the middle of an important regional town of some eighty thousand souls.

The level of the river in Shrewsbury used to fluctuate a lot more than it does now, but early in this century a weir was built across it in Castlefields. The town still floods regularly, but only occasionally is that flooding severe. Even so, there are plans afoot for a new comprehensive flood prevention scheme. This is causing a great deal of concern to conservationists and to many townsfolk. Those for the scheme say it is needed. Those against it say that the barriers, however well landscaped, will change the whole character of the riverside. Only time will tell.

As the river flows over the weir it is heading north once again. Inevitably, near Ditherington, it turns eastwards and then, by the outlying village of Uffington, back towards the south. Until recently the walk along the well-wooded line of the long defunct Shrewsbury Canal from Ditherington to Uffington was a peaceful and pleasant one, following the Severn. From the village, it is a short walk to the dramatically situated ruins of Haughmond Abbey, an Augustinian house noted for the magnificent facade of its twelfth century chapter house. From Uffington also, nearly six hundred years ago, it was a short walk from their camp for Henry the Fourth's army to the field of battle with the rebels.

Uffington itself is a small settlement in the shadow of Haughmond Hill. There was once an eighteenth century sham castle on the brow of the hill. but this fell down in the 1930's. Uffington had its own wharf on the canal, and a rope ferry across the river. By using this ferry, the Owen family of Monkmoor Road, Shrewsbury, reached the small Victorian parish church on Sundays. They preferred its rustic services to those in town. It was whilst walking back from such a service shortly before the First World War that a small event became ingrained in the mind of one of the sons. In the buttercup-rich meadow, Wilfred Owen's boots became covered with golden pollen. A few years later he recaptured the incident in one of his last poems - *Spring Offensive*. Exhausted soldiers rested in a lull in the fighting and the horror of the Western Front:

> *Hour after hour they pondered the warm field*
> *And the far valley behind, where the buttercups*
> *Had blessed with gold, their slow boots coming up.*

Introduction

Winter scene near Haughmond

The Shropshire Severn

The tranquillity of the spot where one of England's greatest war poets once walked has been totally destroyed by the new eastern by-pass. Cars and trucks roar constantly by on the arrow-straight tarmac. To make matters worse, it is one of those ridiculous new type of roads where there are just two very wide lanes - so the more selfish drivers treat it as a four-lane highway. A major disaster is just waiting to happen.

Whilst money gets poured into the road system, the railways continue to be run down. The new road crosses the old railway close to Preston, and the railway, in turn, crosses the river on its original graceful two-span cast iron bridge - now 150 years old. A less obvious, even earlier, and even less well-known, example of transport technology lies nearby. It is almost impossible to spot the Berwick canal tunnel. The obvious place for a tunnel would have been through the base of

The Ferry House and Ferry at Preston Boats around the turn of the century

Introduction

Haughmond Hill - but the Shrewsbury Canal skirted round it. Nevertheless, at Preston Boats, the company though it necessary to dig a tunnel just under one kilometre long. Designed by Josiah Clowes, it was finished in 1796. Dark, damp and narrow, it was only a few feet beneath the ground level. No doubt if it had been built a few years later, the engineers would have made a cutting instead. Today a line of trees and a few air shafts mark its position, and both portals survive.

Back on the river bank close by, Ferry House is a reminder of the rope ferry that crossed just above Preston Boats weir. This was the last of the once numerous fish weirs to survive, finally being swept away earlier this century leaving only the distinctive long and skinny bylet. Fish weirs will be dealt with in more detail later in the book.

Past Emstry the surroundings again take on a well-manicured park-like appearance. This is hardly surprising, as two adjacent estates were landscaped by Humphrey Repton in the early nineteenth century. In the next few miles, there are many architectural gems. These include a pair of very different houses by one of the most famous architects of his day - John Nash. Longner Hall, tucked away in secluded woodlands, was built in 1803 in a very loose neo-Tudor style echoing an English past. Just downstream from Atcham, and built perhaps a year before, is Cronkhill - a little piece of Tuscany transported to the green Shropshire countryside. Claimed to be the first Italianate villa in Britain, it was built by Nash for the agent of the Attingham Park estate and, like Attingham, is now owned by the National Trust.

Attingham Park is perhaps the most famous of Shropshire's great houses. Basically a radical remodelling and extension of an older house, its present form is largely due to George Steuart. Austere, even forbidding, from the outside, the inside is a little too rich for many palates. It was remodelled in this late neo-classical way for Noel Hill, who became Lord Berwick, in the 1780's, and is faced in Grinshill stone. The park, laid out in the valley of the Tern, is famous locally for its deer. Its creation at the end of the eighteenth century also led to radical changes in the village of Atcham. Several of the surviving houses were Romanticised, probably by Nash, to improve the view from the big house.

The village is noted for its three bridges, two over the Severn and one over the Tern, as well as a fine church. This is the only one in the country dedicated to St. Eata, one of the twelve young English boys converted by St. Aidan in the seventh century. He became the first Abbot of Melrose, and later the bishop of Lindisfarne. The name Atcham is possibly derived from Eata. The church

St. Eata's church at Atcham, partly built of Roman stones

Introduction

has Saxon origins and is partly built of Roman masonry quarried from the nearby ruined city of Uriconium. This was also where the monk Ordericus Vitalis was born in the late eleventh century. A noted historian in his day with a style all his own, he lived most of his later life in a monastery in France.

The Tern was once navigable for tiny boats and the remains of a lock can still be seen close to where it joins the Severn. Before Attingham Park was remodelled, there was a large forge here, perhaps the largest in Britain, and it was clearly not the sort of thing any aspiring aristocrat wished to have in his front garden. It was, not surprisingly, demolished.

The Romans first built a fort by the banks of the Severn below Atcham in the first century AD, soon after they conquered Britain. This was then replaced by a large city, the fourth largest in their British dominions. Uriconium became the capital of the local tribe, the Cornovii, and prospered

The lost Roman city of Uriconium (Wroxeter) has fascinated antiquarians for centuries; this is a late-Victorian engraving

until the end of the fourth century. It has fascinated antiquarians and archaeologists for centuries and is now looked after by English Heritage. The most obvious piece of Roman architecture is the 'Old Work', of stone and brick, and the footings of many other buildings have also been excavated.

Yet more exciting discoveries in this vast site remain to be found, but lie protected by the fertile soils that have built up over them. Unfortunately, there have also been isolated incidents of people trespassing on these untouched areas without permission but with metal detectors. Not only do they disturb livestock and trample crops, they plunder our common heritage for personal gain. They also destroy unspectacular but vitally important archaeological information that could enable a better understanding of the past. Fines, even if these common thieves are caught, remain derisory.

The modern village of Wroxeter occupies only a small part of Uriconium. Its large church, St. Andrew's, like that of Atcham, is built largely of re-used Roman masonry and its gateway is flanked by Roman columns. The church was a Saxon foundation, rebuilt after the Norman Conquest.

Overlooking the whole valley from the east is Shropshire's best-known landmark, the Wrekin. Although not a particularly high hill, it rises steeply from the plain and has that well-known beached whale shape familiar to all Salopians. One of the many legends associated with it tells of a Welsh giant who had fallen out with the people of Shrewsbury. He decided to take a load of earth in his huge spade and dam the Severn, thus flooding the town. Losing his way, he met a cobbler carrying a sack of old worn shoes that needed mending. Asking the cobbler for directions, he let slip his devious plan. The cobbler, anxious not to lose such valued customers, declared that Shrewsbury was many arduous miles away - and that he had worn out all the shoes in his bag just by walking from there. Tired and hungry, the giant gave up, dumped the earth where he stood, scraped the mud off his spade, and walked home. The result was the Wrekin, and its outlier, the Ercall.

A little over a mile below Wroxeter the river is joined on its west side by the Cound Brook. The village from which it takes its name boasts one of the finest small country houses of the Queen Anne period, Cound Hall. Built in 1704 by John Prince of Shrewsbury, but influenced by the more famous architect, Francis Smith of Warwick, it is an example of the toned-down English version of the Baroque. A little further downstream, Cound Lodge Inn may have been the dower house of Cound, and bears the date 1750. The house faces the river; indeed, it is virtually on the river bank. The two gables facing the main road are part of the rear elevation.

Introduction

The restored belvidere at Eyton-on-Severn

On the ridge of higher land on the north side of the river, and much less well known than either of these houses, is a fragment of a once imposing mansion. Eyton-on-Severn lies on a quiet back lane. Here lived Lord Herbert of Chirbury, a famous philosopher and statesman. Only a garden belvidere and fragments of wall remain of the brick mansion begun by Sir Francis Newport in 1607, but traces of a matching belvidere survive in the farmhouse. The belvidere has been restored by the Vivat Trust in 1984 and is let out as a holiday home. On the watermeadows below the ridge is the Eyton Point-to-Point racecourse, a very popular venue on racedays, evoking the old days of horse-racing long before the arrival of huge stadia and computerised betting.

Until the end of the eighteenth century there were no bridges across the river between Atcham and Buildwas. Then Telford built a timber toll bridge at Cressage, replaced early this century by one of reinforced concrete. The village is pleasant enough but has few remarkable features. The view from the bridge towards the Wrekin, though, is one of the set-pieces on the Severn. The village claims to take its name from Christ's Oak, and is one of several places where St. Augustine is supposed to have preached beneath an oak tree. There is, inevitably, a revered Christ's Oak today, said to be a descendant of the original. The church is a Victorian one of little note, but it replaced a medieval one nearer to the river that kept getting flooded out.

Past Cressage it becomes apparent that the river valley is not widening out, as it would be expected to do. Instead the valley sides are closing in. The reasons for this will be explained in a later chapter, but the result is one of the most spectacular stretches of river scenery in all England. This begins at Leighton, a small village of several neat estate cottages, some of considerable

Introduction

The Wrekin from Cressage Bridge

antiquity, and Leighton Hall, set in pretty riverside parkland and dating to 1778. In this village was born the Shropshire novelist, Mary Webb. Immediately to the south is Leighton bank, an outrider of the Wrekin, and from the lay-byes on the top is another of the picture-postcard views of the river. Below, in the water meadows, the Severn twists and turns in the famous Leighton 'Crooked-'S'', or 'Horseshoe'. In winter, the whole valley can look like a lake during the floods.

On the opposite side of the river on a narrow lane lies the tiny village of Sheinton. A little further downstream is Buildwas, the village on what is now the north bank, the more famous abbey on the south bank, close to the bridge. Founded in 1135 by the Bishop of Coventry and Lichfield for monks of the Savigny order, it, and they, were taken over by the powerful Cistercians in 1147. The buildings that survive were probably put up shortly after this date and Buildwas is one of the

Buildwas Abbey, one of the finest examples of late-Norman work in the country

most complete and relatively unaltered examples of its date. It was built at a time when the no-nonsense Norman style of architecture was beginning to change into the more decorative Gothic - the resultant mix now known as Transitional. Buildwas presents a fine picture from the higher ground off the road towards Much Wenlock. Close up, the ruined arcades of the nave and chancel are very impressive, but pride of place must go to the vaulted Chapter House. The rib-vaulting at Buildwas is some of the earliest in the country.

The monks of Buildwas were the first industrialists in the area, six centuries before the Industrial Revolution. They used the river to export wool from their flocks grazing on the surrounding fields, and also to carry coal mined from beneath those fields - though coal only became an important heating fuel in the later sixteenth century. The abbey also controlled the bridge crossing over the Severn. The medieval bridge was virtually destroyed by floods at the end of the eighteenth century, and Telford built his first iron bridge to replace it. That has long since been taken down.

This is not the bridge of a 1930's ocean liner - but the main control of Ironbridge 'A' power station when new

Introduction

As the valley sides close in even more, the natural tranquility of the scenery is shattered by one of the most unsympathetically sited buildings of the 1960's - the Ironbridge B power station. Ironbridge A, built just before the Second World War, was bad enough. Ironbridge B is an aesthetic accident, with its huge steaming cooling towers crowded into the wooded confines at the head of the gorge. In the flat featureless expanses of the lower Trent valley, these clusters of curve-sided towers take on a clumsy grace and punctuate the views in a manner that is almost attractive, but not here. This coal-fired monstrosity is also accused by enviromentalists of being a considerable source of pollution and of acid rain. It does have two things in its favour: it provides local jobs, and it has the decency to be served mainly by rail - a branch line being specially kept open to serve it. That line, in turn, has saved the graceful Albert Edward Bridge carrying it over the river.

Beyond the power station the real drama of the Severn valley begins - for this is the start of the Ironbridge Gorge. This natural crease in the countryside is a result of the last ice-age and has resulted in a romantic landscape of steep wooded cliffs towering above the river on both sides. It is also a somewhat unstable landscape, demonstrated most astonishingly by the great landslip of 1773. Roughly opposite the site of the power station, on the 27th May of that year, the bank began to give way over a broad front. The sliding earth moved the turnpike road and completely blocked the Severn, causing chaos to the navigation and to the surrounding farmland. The river quickly cut itself a new channel. The renowned local preacher, William Fletcher of Madeley, seized on the event for the topic of one of his fire-and-brimstone sermons.

The Ironbridge Gorge is now so well known there is little new that can be written about it. Every schoolchild in Britain now knows that this was the cradle of the Industrial Revolution that has shaped - for better or for worse - our modern world. It is, not surprisingly, a World Heritage Site. The major innovation that took place here was to do with the smelting of iron. Before Abraham Darby arrived in the area at the start of the eighteenth century, the fuel used in iron smelting was charcoal - a severely limited resource despite the use of coppiced woodlands. This area had all the raw materials needed for iron production - the iron ore, the timber, and the limestone used as flux in the process. In the steep-sided Coalbrookdale the Cole Brook provided water power to blow the bellows. The river provided the vital transport link. Darby, however, was interested in another local raw material in his experiments - coal. In 1709 he managed to use coke to smelt iron, instead of charcoal. The process took a little while to get right, but when it was finally reliable enough, a major breakthrough had been made. No longer were the ironmasters reliant on the

Beneath the glass pyramid is Coalbrookdale's 'old furnace' where Abraham Darby first smelted iron with coke. The train on the viaduct takes coal to Ironbridge Power Station.

limited quantities of charcoal - they could use the virtually unlimited supplies of coal. As a result, the price of producing iron came down, along with the cost of iron goods.

The colliery district of this part of Shropshire had a head start on the rest of the country and thrived for a century or more as one of the most important industrial areas in Europe. Darby's was only one of a series of iron-related 'firsts' in the Gorge. The first iron bridge (or rather, the first major iron bridge) of 1779 gave its name to Ironbridge and is world famous, rightly so. Here too, in an area where there had been wooden railways since the start of the seventeenth century, were made the first iron railway wheels (by 1729), the first iron rails (1767), and, though unsuccessful, the first railway locomotive (1802). On the river itself in 1787 the first successful iron boat, the *Trial*, was launched by John 'Iron-Mad' Wilkinson at Willey wharf. What other place in the world can boast so many important innovations in such a short time and in such a small area?

Introduction

Even in the eighteenth century, tourists came to the Gorge to view the splendours of the modern world. Industry and innovation were seen as heroic. The image was no doubt helped by the fact that so many of the areas where industries were being developed were as picturesque as the Gorge. The reality of industrialisation was, of course, very different, and the dramatic furnace fires so loved by the rich visitors passing through Ironbridge or Coalbrookdale were soon playing their part in destroying the local environment and polluting the lives of those who had to work in and amongst them.

Now that Nature, with a little help from the preservationists and planners, is reclaiming her own, the setting of both Gorge and Dale befits that of a major visitor attraction. The well-kept houses of Ironbridge cling to terraces on the steep wooded hillside in picturesque abandon. Shops sell the things that tourists like to buy, and the air is clean. Tourists once again flock to the Gorge, but this time in unprecedented numbers. They come to see the bridge, of course, and the many fine industrial museums run by the Ironbridge Gorge Museum Trust. But what they see is a sanitized version of the past, tidied-up and clothed with a genteel veil of nostalgia. This version is all that we can ever see. It is impossible really to envisage what it was like to work and suffer in those ironworks or coal mines, to feel the pain of the sheer hard physical labour of twelve hour shifts six days a week, or taste the sulphur in the atmosphere. The ruins of that past are preserved with a care and reverence once reserved only for castles, cathedrals and great houses. The lives of the people are mainly seen in fading sepia photographs, barren statistics, and a rich oral history.

The Severn was the life blood of this industrial past, for reasons explained in later chapters. It was the transport artery that brought in the raw materials and took out the finished goods and the coal. There are a few obvious reminders of its role. The Loadcroft warehouse, a castellated folly of the 1840's, stands by the river and still has the troughs in its sloping wharf to mark the route of the iron plateways that brought goods to the waiting barges. It now, appropriately, houses a Museum of the River. There are fragments of other old wharves here and there but very little else.

Down in the Gorge on the crowded riverside, it is difficult to see that this is now part of a New Town much larger than Shrewsbury. Just over the ridge above Ironbridge the estates of houses and industrial units begin, all linked by roads and roundabouts. Telford New Town was set up in the 1960's. It was designed to take overspill from the West Midlands and to link up the gradually decaying industrial towns of East Shropshire - Wellington, Madeley, and Oakengates. Some like it,

The Shropshire Severn

Ironbridge

Introduction

some loathe it. Some praise it for regenerating the region, some blame it for the decay of the centres of the older towns. Whatever its merits, it is here to stay.

Equally unknown to most of the tourists in the Gorge are the settlements up on top of the south side of the Gorge. The main carpark may be on the old station site on the opposite end of the iron bridge, but few venture up the steep slope towards Broseley or Benthall. That is their loss. Benthall has a fine Elizabethan mansion, surrounded by lovely gardens and opened by the National Trust. Broseley is a small Georgian town in its own right with several good brick houses, a unique clay-tobacco pipe works soon to be opened as a museum, and one or two steep tracks, or jitties, running down the slope to the river.

Downstream from Ironbridge, although still flowing within its gorge, the river enters a quieter region - despite allowing itself a little juvenile fun at the rapids below the Jackfield Free Bridge. There are still museums here, on either side, but only the more discerning visitors make their way to the Coalport China Works, or the Craven Dunhill pottery in Jackfield. The scenery here, if anything, is wilder. Off the road and down by the tree-fringed river, it is not too difficult to believe you are on the banks of the Amazon as the brown sluggish water flows by. There are scars of industry in these river-side woods too, the odd broken brick wall here, or the constantly cascading screes of millions of tile 'wasters'.

Running down to the south side of the river are several hidden wooded valleys, or dingles, pleasant places to walk in. It was down valleys such as these that the earliest wooden railways - or waggonways - were built hundreds of years before Stephenson's Rocket. Throughout the Gorge the land is unstable. The Severn Valley Railway were always having problems, and on occasion saw their tracks swept away by landslides. Roads have fared no better. On the south bank, fragments of the old road past Jackfield can be seen in the undergrowth, having slid down the bank. The little traffic there is now has to use a specially built 'carpet' of planks.

The industrial Gorge comes to an end at another New Town, Coalport. There was once virtually nothing here. Towards the end of the eighteenth century it was chosen as the terminus of one arm of the Shropshire Canal. A quite amazing inclined plane linked the canal at river level with that on the top of the slope. The Hay Incline has been partially restored to give some idea of the sheer audacity of the design. Within a few years, Coalport was one of the most important ports on the river, and also had a famous china works, warehouses, and the remarkable Tar Tunnel.

Introduction

Coalport Bridge, painted by J. H. Smith, who worked as an artist at the Coalport China Factory in the nineteenth century

A completely new settlement had grown up purely because of the arrival of the canal.

The Severn valley between Coalport and Bridgnorth is one of the most peaceful, and least known, stretches on the whole river. No roads intrude on its quietude, no traffic destroys its tranquillity. The woods and cliffs of the Gorge continue but are no longer scarred by traces of industry. This was not always the case. In the eighteenth century there was an important china works at Caughley on the higher ground not far from the south bank; its wares are now collectors' items. Apley Park is one of overlooked treasures of the county, a somewhat eccentric Gothick mansion mainly built in 1811. It is set in picture-book parkland overlooking the Severn, and close by is the tree-cloaked sandstone cliff of the oddly named Apley Terrace. The river here is crossed, surprisingly, by a graceful steel suspension bridge, built by the one-time owners of the mansion to provide private access to the railway station on the other side of the river.

Just upstream of Bridgnorth, the wooded cliffs on the east bank continuing the line of Apley Terrace are breached by the River Worfe - the 'wandering Worfe' that drains much of eastern

Near Coalport

Apley Park, taken from a battlemented bridge on the disused part of the Severn Valley Railway

Shropshire. A mill race taken off this river just before it joins the Severn powered the waterwheels of the castellated Fort Pendleston, actually a nineteenth century carpet factory. The cliffs continue past Bridgnorth itself. The soft nature of the rock allowed, in times gone by, people to burrow into them for refuge or for accommodation - and the best known of these cave dwellings is the Hermitage on the top of the rocks opposite the town. This was the legendary retreat of Ethelward, a brother of King Athelstan and grandson of Alfred the Great. He cared only for literature, and not for riches, and spent most of his life in this secluded spot. People lived in cliff dwellings in this part of the Severn valley right up until the nineteenth century, and later still in neighbouring parts of Staffordshire on Kinver Edge.

The regimented trees and razor-cut grass on the west bank of the river herald the approach of Bridgnorth - they belong to its golf course. Perched on the edge of a sandstone cliff on the edge of the Severn, the town has to have one of the most dramatic sites in England. In the nineteenth century, writers were keen to compare the town's setting with a variety of exotic locations, such as

Introduction

Jerusalem, or even Gibraltar. Such parallels are a little far fetched. It certainly has, from a distance, a Continental flavour reminiscent of those hilltop towns of Italy or Spain. Its topography has divided it in two. The main part, or High Town, is laid out on top of the plateau with a church at either end. Houses tumble down the cliffside towards Low Town, occupying both banks of the river and once the commercial and industrial heart of one of the most important river ports in the country. The two parts were, until 1792, linked only by narrow stepped alleyways - again the feel of the Mediterranean fringe - and a single precipitous zig-zag road for wheeled traffic, the Cartway.

Despite all this, Bridgnorth is a quintessential English market town, and a busy one at that. There is some confusion as to its origins - and it is either here or at Quatford that the first bridge over the

Near Apley

The Shropshire Severn

Bridgnorth

Introduction

Shropshire Severn was built in the ninth century. Fortified as one of the burhs of Aethelflaeda, Lady of the Mercians, it was usurped by Quatford after the Norman Conquest. A short time later, the owner of Quatford, Robert de Beleme, rebelled against the king, decided that the site of Bridgnorth was easier to defend, and built his castle here. The town quickly developed in its shadow.

It has a wealth of fine buildings, from timber-framed merchant houses to the elegant Georgian houses of mellow brick lining East Castle Street. Of particular note are Bishop Percy's house at the bottom of Cartway, a triple-gabled timber-framed house of 1580, and two early seventeenth century brick buildings - the Governor's Lodge in East Castle Street and the former Grammar School by St. Leonard's church. The churches at either end of High Town are very different in character but, to all intents, not dissimilar in age and not that ancient. The red sandstone Gothic of St. Leonard's, beautifully sited on its own green, is largely a Victorian rebuilding of the original - by William Slater in 1862. The old church dated back to Norman times but was badly damaged during the Civil War. The Roundheads had taken the town in 1646 but had to besiege the castle. St. Leonard's was used as a stronghold by the attackers and was fired on by the Royalists in the castle at the opposite end of High Town. Much of the town between was badly damaged in the process.

The church of St. Mary Magdalene was built in the castle bailey in 1792 in grey stone and a neo-classical style drawn up by an amateur architect - the great civil engineer Thomas Telford. It replaced the old castle chapel. All that remains of the castle are the Governor's Lodge, and the Norman keep. The keep is Bridgnorth's version of the Leaning Tower of Pisa. After the castle finally surrendered, it was deliberately pulled down, or 'slighted' by the Roundheads. Attempts to reduce the keep to rubble by blowing it up failed, leaving its remains on a lean of 17 degrees. It has looked as if it is about to topple ever since. The rest of the castle site was built over in the eighteenth century. The views from the Castle Terrace over the Severn valley are wonderful - marred a little now by the new by-pass bridge and its approaches striding across the valley floor to the south. There is much to see in the streets of the town as well, and Bridgnorth is one of those places that rewards the patient explorer with pleasant surprises round many a corner.

Leaning on the balustrade of Bridgnorth bridge and looking over at the shallows, it is difficult to picture the once busy quays that lined the Severn when barges had to wait their turn to unload. It is perhaps even more difficult to realise that ocean-going ships were once built here in this inland

Bridgnorth's Cliff Railway - the steepest inland line in Britain

Introduction

town. Most of the boatyards in Bridgnorth, along with the other Shropshire boatyards, built river-going craft. Larger ones were occasionally built here to order for use around the coast or on the open sea. The *Severn*, a 166 ton brig built of oak and ash in 1850, traded to the Baltic. The 135-ton *Gleaner*, another brig built in 1855, was fully sheathed in zinc, classed A1 at Lloyds, and sailed as far as South America and the West Indies. Bridgnorth-built boats could also be long-lasting. Another *Severn*, a schooner-rigged vessel of 71 tons, was trading out of Carrickfergus in the 1880's and was said to have been built in Bridgnorth in 1752!

A simple plaque in Low Town, at the east end of the bridge, is a reminder of Bridgnorth's role in the history of another form of transport. It was on this site, then occupied by William Hazeldine's foundry, that John Raistrick built, to a Richard Trevithick design, the world's first passenger locomotive in 1808. The *Catch-me-who-can* was taken down to London and people paid to watch this amazing new invention run round a circular track in Euston. The more adventurous could ride on the carriage it pulled, and thus became the first to pay for a steam powered railway journey. After a few weeks the novelty wore off, a rail broke, and the venture folded. Bridgnorth has still got other railway 'claims to fame' - the only inland cliff railway in the country, linking Low and High Town since 1892, and, of course, one of the best preserved steam railways in the world - the Severn Valley Railway.

For the rest of its journey through the county, the Severn is accompanied by the nostalgic sights, sounds and smells of the steam train era. The Severn Valley line, built with great difficulty in the unstable terrain of the valley at the start of the 1860's, has followed the river since it left Shrewsbury. Apart from a few stations converted to private houses, long sections of disused and overgrown cuttings, and the remains of bridges and embankments, there has been little to see. The same fate has happened to thousands of miles of branch lines since the 1960's, and could well have happened to the rest of the Severn Valley line after it closed in 1963. However, a band of enthusiasts pulled together to buy the track from Bridgnorth to Hampton Loade. A short section opened in 1970, and since then the line has been extended, in stages, to as far as the main British Rail line at Kidderminster. A regular service of steam-hauled trains, professionally run by amateurs, takes the traveller back to the past throughout the summer months.

The river continues to run in a deep-sided trough in the rolling topography of south-eastern Shropshire. A mile or two away from the river, on either side of it, there is little in the landscape to

A Severn Valley Railway train leaves Highley, heading for Kidderminster

indicate that the river even exists. The views stretch westwards to the Clee Hills and beyond, and eastwards across the Midland Plain. The river seems to be slipping stealthily through the landscape without being seen.

Immediately to the south of Bridgnorth on the west bank is Panpudding Hill, often considered to be the true site of the Saxon burh, and from where Parliamentarian canon bombarded the castle. A little further on is Daniel's Mill, set in a steep little valley. Its millpond feeds a tall, spindly waterwheel, 31 foot high, cast at Coalbrookdale in 1834, and probably the tallest still working in the country. It makes the most of the limited water available; the mill, recently restored, is open to the public.

Introduction

On the opposite bank, past the caravan sites, Quatford has a setting almost as dramatic as that of Bridgnorth itself. It would be a much better place if the busy A442 did not run straight, and swiftly, through it. The Norman motte-and-bailey castle stood on a rocky bluff overlooking the river. Its modern castle, a little to the north of the village, is a gargantuan embattled pile high in the wooded hillside, built by John Smalman, a local builder, in 1830. He also built a smaller watch-tower in the village itself, and possibly remodelled some of its houses. The church, though largely rebuilt in the early eighteenth century, has a romantic tale attached to it. Countess Adelisa, wife of Roger de

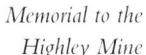
Memorial to the Highley Mine

Montgomery, first Earl of Shrewsbury, was caught in a storm in the English Channel on the way to see her husband. As the ship was being battered by the elements, she vowed that, if she survived, she would pay for a church to be built on the spot when she first saw her husband again; that spot was at Quatford.

At Eardington there are the remains of a small industrial complex, Lower Forge, close to the river, and there was once a wharf. To it came iron from the Gorge area to be worked on hearths at the Lower Forge and the Upper Forge, a little higher up the valley of the Mor Brook. Only fragments of brick wall survive buried in deep undergrowth. Nearby is Chelmarsh reservoir, used for sailing as well as for water supply. The Mor Brook joins the Severn opposite the parkland surrounding Dudmaston Hall, a Victorianised Georgian house now opened by the National Trust. Further south, a mile or so from the river, is Quatt, a village of late-Victorian mock-half-timbered estate cottages, but with a fine Georgian church and the dower house of Dudmaston next to it.

Near Highley

The picturesque riverside village of Hampton Loade still has its rope ferry, summoned these days not by a 'holler' from the bank but by an electric bell. There used not to be bridges between Bridgnorth and Bewdley, so these ferries were once important. This one remained so when the village's railway station was built on the wrong side of the river. It is a popular place in summer, reached by foot, by road, or rail, and the ferry is still well used.

Downstream of Hampton Loade it is a little difficult now to realise that there were two large collieries, one on either bank, until just over twenty years ago. Both sites are now being reclaimed as part of the Severn Valley Country Park, and only on closer inspection does the nature of the ground and the as yet immature planting betray the recent landscaping. On the west bank is Highley, until the end of the last century a tiny village with its Norman church and handful of timber-framed or brick cottages. Then came coal. A new mining village, complete with rows of terraced colliers' houses, grew up next to the old village, and a slightly later addition was then built at nearby Woodhill. The colliery itself lay between the village and the river and had sidings on the Severn Valley line. Later, new workings sprang up between the east bank of the river and Alveley. This is stone country and there were quarries here in the past. The village boasts several good stone houses and a fine, if heavily restored, church. It managed to escape the fate of Highley and retained its rural character.

Alveley and Highley are the last of the Shropshire villages on the Severn, and beyond them the river flows on through still silvan scenery into Worcestershire. Just as the river seemed reluctant to enter the county, balancing on the Welsh border for a mile or so, it seems reluctant to leave. For the last mile the county border again follows the river and then, a little distance beyond the confluence of the Borle Brook, the Severn leaves Shropshire behind. Downstream the scenery remains picturesque until Worcester, from thereon becoming simply pleasant all the way to the estuary. Nowhere else, though, is the valley as varied as it is in Shropshire, the county with which the river is synonymous to so many people. Sabrina and Salopia just seem to go together.

Tommy Rogers, one of the great characters of the river. His descendants keep the tradition alive

The Coracle

By far the smallest, but most distinctive, of all the Severn craft is the coracle. Its origins are lost in time, but it was certainly in use by the Saxon period. A 1645 description also gives the reason for the name. It was *'a little boate for one to sitte in; they call them corricles, laths within and leather without, from corium.'* *'Corium'* is the Latin for an animal hide.

Although learning to control a coracle is a little like riding a bicycle on water, in the hands of the expert they are very manoeuvrable, versatile and virtually silent. They were ideal for fishing, the odd bit of poaching, or simply for crossing from one side of the river to the other.

Their greatest advantage over any other craft is their light weight. A 1704 description of Rossall, near Shrewsbury, explains. *'Here are small Fishing-boats, call'd Coracles, of an oval Figure, made of Twigs interwoven, covered over with an Ox-hide, so light, that the Fisher-men carry 'em home upon their Shoulders.'* Coracles are, and were, not unique to the Severn and there were many different variations. Even earlier this century, for example, the Shrewsbury coracles were slightly different from those of Ironbridge.

Although not designed for anything but the shortest of journeys, a Shropshire octagenarian is said to have paddled his coracle all the way to Worcester in the 1790's. Mr Peplow wanted to see George the Third, who was visiting that city. How he got back to Shropshire is not recorded!

The ancient tradition of coracle-making is still being kept alive as a craft in the Ironbridge Gorge to this day. Whilst some still build them in the traditional way, with twigs and hide, the space-age coracle is made of specially sawn timber and calico cloth.

The Shropshire Severn

The Physical Background

There may never have been a Shropshire Severn as we know it at all - the original river ran from the Welsh hills northwards to the Dee estuary. David Pannett explains the river's geological background, and shows how the Ice Ages changed its course and produced the present landscape of its valley.

Many people who learned about rivers in their school geography lessons may find the River Severn rather confusing - it seems to flow the wrong way round! It enters the county meandering over a broad alluvial plain and then leaves it through a narrow gorge. The explanation lies in the Ice Ages.

Right: The Severn near Melverley, looking upstream to the Breidden hills

Left: The Leighton Horseshoe, or meanders

A mini ice age - the frozen Severn in Shropshire in Shrewsbury in 1963

Several times during the last five million years, vast ice sheets have built up over Wales and northern Britain, invading the North Shropshire Plain from the west and north respectively. However, as each cold period tended to destroy the evidence of earlier episodes, it is only to the most recent that we can really look to find out the reasons for today's visible features. Appropriately enough that last glaciation is now called by geologists the Devensian - because the landscape produced by it can be so well seen in the Shropshire-Cheshire Plain. *Deva* was the Roman name for Chester.

Cold conditions, with an associated fall in sea-level and increased erosion, probably gripped this region some forty thousand years ago, but it was perhaps not until twenty thousand years ago that the ice sheets arrived. A great glacier poured down the upper Severn valley from the Welsh Ice Cap. Close to Shrewsbury it converged with an even more powerful one coming from the Irish

The Physical Background

Sea. Each brought with them their own characteristic 'erratic stones' - that is, stones broken off the land many miles away and carried in the glacier to be deposited where the glaciers stopped. These included grey mudstones from Wales and pink granites from the Lake District and the Scottish Borders, all mixed with the locally eroded soft sandstones.

The two glaciers filled the plain, pressed against the surrounding hills, and over-rode the watershed of the Wenlock Edge and the East Shropshire coalfield to enter the headwaters of the lower Severn and the Stour. The ice advance finally came to rest at Eardington, south of Bridgnorth. From there meltwater and gravely sediment spread down the valley in a typical 'outwash train'. At the same time similar drainage into the headwaters of the Teme took place through the hills at Church Stretton, where the ice was pressed between the Long Mynd and Caer Caradoc.

As can be seen at the snout of any modern glacier, summer melting is not confined to the visible ice front, but takes place over a very wide area of the surface. This melted water then disappears into crevasses and ice caves to emerge at the 'snout' as a ready formed river. In the Shropshire

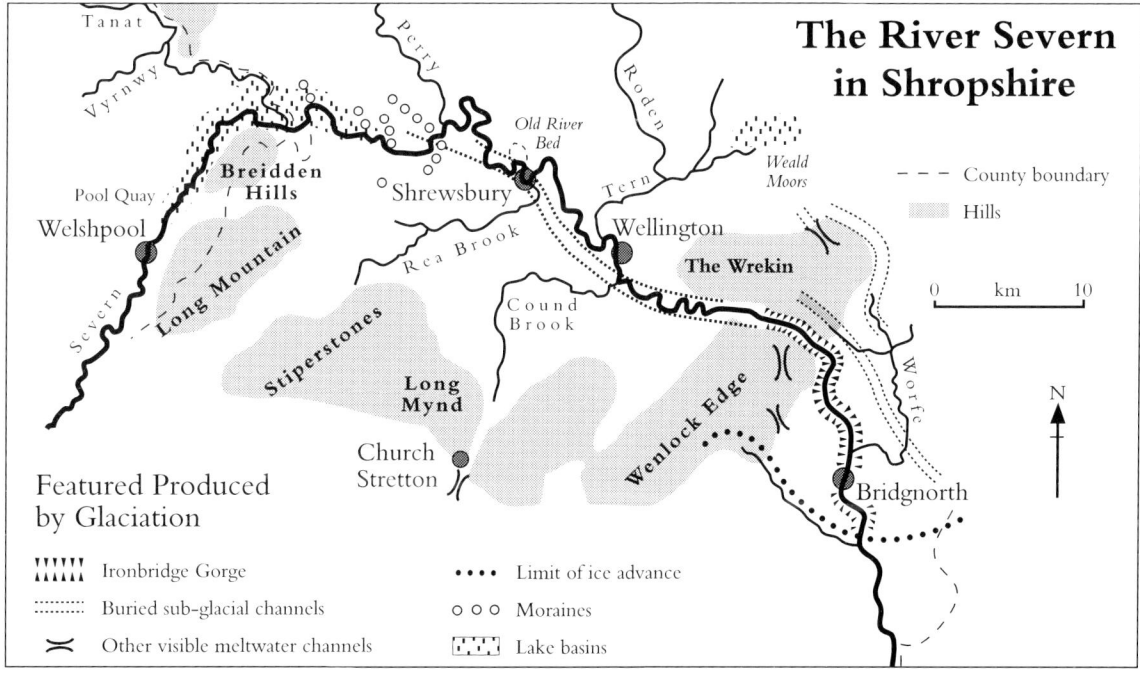

glacier, the encircling hills also immobilised the bottom - or basal - layers of the ice so that only the surface layers could slide forward over the top. In any case such a 'polar' ice sheet would normally be so frozen to the ground that it could only move by internal deformation - in contrast to the down-hill sliding of a typical 'alpine' glacier. The result of all this stability was that the internal meltwater streams cut a whole network of channels into the bedrock of the Shropshire-Cheshire Plain. These sometimes also show their apparent ability to flow uphill and downhill under the hydrostatic 'head' provided by the thick ice cover above.

In this way several channels crossed over the Wenlock watershed. As the ice receded, allowing water to take an easier surface route, these channels were back-filled with sand and gravel and lost from sight. Only the channel near Ironbridge took more and more of the flow and cut itself deeper and deeper to the create the present steep-sided gorge. By this time the ice front had receded northwards into the Shropshire Plain, and this new valley was draining the area - by gravity - very close to present levels.

Downstream, rapid incision left the old 'outwash train' surviving as a terrace high up on each side of the valley around Bridgnorth and Eardington. Upstream, the old subglacial part of the channel was at first filled in with glacial deposits. Later, from Cound downstream, these were cleared out again by the new river - so that only fragments remain at Buildwas.

Such glacial deposits in a rock-cut valley descending westwards are the clearest evidence for a subglacial origin of this part of the gorge. However, they were a great puzzle to the late Professor Wills when he suggested that the gorge had been formed by the overflow of the huge lake left by the retreating ice. Whilst such a lake must have been formed during the initial advance of the ice, it is clear that the melting in the plain involved a chaotic pattern of stagnant ice masses between which there were many local lakes and outwash plains - all draining through the new gorge. In general, drainage tended to follow the previous sub-glacial lines, but upstream of Cound the Severn had to establish a twisting route to one side of the sand and gravels. It crossed the boulder clays of the decaying ice and even cut into solid sandstone in places. Only through boreholes can the old channel - termed the 'Severn Trench' by water engineers - be traced westwards. As it passes under the centre of Shrewsbury, modern builders have become well aware of the problems it can pose. For instance, the new Darwin Centre stands on thirty metre deep piles! The existence of this soft sediment also caused the town to shake during the Clun earthquake of 1990.

Ironbridge Gorge

The Shropshire Severn

The Shrewsbury area had long been a sort of battle ground between the Welsh and Irish Sea ice sheets, but as the latter decayed the Welsh one appears to have surged forward - over-riding both sediments and stagnant ice blocks, burying them all beneath a new layer. Only when the climate had become much warmer and the Welsh ice had disappeared did some of the buried blocks of ice finally melt, producing craters known as kettle holes. The existence of wider sheets of dead ice in hollows no doubt helped the Severn to cut across those small sandstone hills at Kingsland and between Preston Boats and Emstrey as it made its new valley. Meltwaters also spread out an 'outwash train' down the Rea Brook and into the Severn Valley - which today form the extensive gravel terraces around Meole Brace, Monkmoor and Uffington.

Soon, however, the ice front retreated again. It stopped long enough to build up a clear crescent-shaped terminal moraine around Montford Bridge. Below this the Severn incised a wide meandering channel into the older deposits towards Shrewsbury. Some of these were very soft sands filling the old subglacial trench. As a result the river bends became particularly pronounced - especially around the appropriately named Isle estate, where the narrow neck of the loop is only a few hundred yards across. A similarly tight bend was later cut off by the river to create the so-called Old River Bed in Shrewsbury, whilst another provided the county town's natural defensive site.

Further retreats, pauses and perhaps temporary new advances of the Welsh glacier then left two smaller moraines from Shrawardine to Ensdon and at Felton Butler. These are 'textbook' examples that can be clearly seen by travellers along the new A5.

Meanwhile, where the glacier emerged from the confines of the Welsh hills, it had been excavating a deep hollow in the soft sandstones of the plain, reaching to below sea-level in places and trimming back the steep faces of the Breidden and Nesscliffe hills. The scene must once have looked like one of the modern glaciers draining the Greenland ice cap, but as the ice melted back the exposed hollow became a lake - not unlike those of the English Lake District. In its still waters up to fifty metres of clay slowly settled - under modern Pentre and Melverley - whilst at the western end deltas of sand and gravel spread out from the Welsh valleys at Llanymynech, Four Crosses and Arddleen.

Eventually, the combined effects of this filling in, and of the erosion at the outlet through the moraines, drained the lake. Even today, in times of flood, it can reappear temporarily - and additional layers of river silt are spread over the clay. Since the eighteenth and nineteenth centuries

The Physical Background

much of the wetter areas have been protected by flood banks, locally known as argae after the Welsh term for a barrier. As a result the area has lost much of its natural ability to absorb dangerous floods - and no doubt all this has exaggerated the peaks and troughs of river flows further downstream.

River channels in deep silt and clay tend to be deep and narrow, whilst those in gravel tend to be wide and shallow. On the Severn the change from one to another may have determined the traditional limits of navigation on the Vyrnwy below Llanymynech and on the Severn at Pool Quay.

As the last Ice Age finally began to give way, tundra vegetation clothed the land and bound the topsoil - as it still does in the Artic Circle parts of Russia for example. Rates of erosion and deposition were reduced and further evolution of the Severn valley slowed down. Nevertheless, cool wet conditions and spring snow melt kept the actual river channel large. However, as the climate became, for a time, even milder and drier than today, all rivers shrank and backfilled surplus channel capacity with fine silt, helped by dense alder and willow woodlands. Since the clearance of forest we now see this sediment as belts of alluvial floodplain about twice the width of the present river - occupying at least two-thirds of its original late-Glacial channel.

Aerial view of Wroxeter, showing the distinctive bylet that marks the site of a former fish weir

About five thousand years ago, when the river had already ceased to change its channel much more, it nevertheless managed to cut off the Old River Bed at Shrewsbury. An answer to this contradiction must lie in those particularly soft and easily erodable sandy deposits filling the subglacial trench and in a conveniently sited kettle hole that the river could exploit. Other kettle holes pock-mark the area and their relationship to the valley suggests that they may have still been in the process of collapse when it was being formed originally.

The clue to the date of the cut-off comes from pollen grains preserved in the muds and peats that built up in the 'ox-bow lake'. They show a mixed deciduous forest containing oak, hazel, and also lime - the main clue. Thereafter the pollen frequency reflected both the evolution of the lake into a marsh and the modification of forest by man. Eventually so much land had been cleared that eroded soil washed into the peat. This situation is also reflected in the topmost layers of floodplain silt along the main river. Whilst the lower layers appear to be made up of fine recycled glacial deposits, the particles above show chemical changes produced by having once weathered in a soil. Almost a metre overlies the Roman surfaces of Wroxeter and the foundations of the Roman bath-house at Lea Cross in the Rea Valley are likewise buried suggesting a Medieval date for this soil erosion. Otherwise layers within the floodplain are hard to find or date because it was constantly turned over by earthworms as it slowly built up to its present two or three metre thickness.

Although each flood adds a little more silt to the floodplain, this is not evenly distributed. Most builds up on the actual river bank to form a natural levee - leaving the further areas as a lower 'backswamp'. Where the river has managed to shift its channel sideways by eroding one bank, successive old levees may be left behind on the opposite side of the floodplain leaving clues to its growth. Their shape parallel to a curving river has earned them the name 'scroll bars'. Other undulations may, however, be the result of medieval cultivation, where villages with ample supplies of natural meadow land also used the floodplain for arable fields. Where these survive they are further clues to the antiquity of the surface of the floodplain. Unfortunately, the renewed drive towards arable cultivation in recent decades has not only disturbed traditional meadow flora but has also erased some of these natural and archaeological features.

In general, rising and falling floods still show up clearly the slightest relief pattern on apparently fairly level surfaces. Such analysis of the floodplain opposite Wroxeter suggested that much of it was old and therefore very little could have been eroded from the cliff below the Roman city over many centuries - and this was later confirmed by archaeologists finding remains of its defences still on the lip.

Floodplains, of course, usually give a river the opportunity of developing meanders by alternately eroding and depositing along its banks. However, the degree to which the Severn displays textbook meandering is much less than it may appear at a quick glance at the map.

The Shropshire Severn

The steep valley sides of the Ironbridge Gorge caused the engineers of the Severn Valley Railway problems for a century. Opposite Dale End they resorted to building a half-viaduct into the bank

Preston Boats Fish Weir was the last to survive, finally being dismantled earlier this century

the town's eighteenth century water supply system and its waterwheel.

Other braided sites were very useful for fish weirs, since the weir fence could block one channel leaving another free for navigation. More often, however, an artificial 'braid' - the barge gutter - was created around the weir. Many of the typical long islands produced survive along the course of the river - including ones at Little Shrawardine, Montford, Castlefields (Shrewsbury), Pimley, Preston Boats, Wroxeter and Bridgnorth. Several others have since been fused with the flood plain and the old gutters only show up in times of flood - as at Eaton Constantine, Eye Manor and Dudmaston. There is a particularly good example of natural braiding and an abandoned barge gutter just upstream from Atcham Bridge, often mistaken for an 'ox-bow' lake. In the Ironbridge gorge area some riffles contain a large proportion of industrial debris as well as natural rocks slumping in from the unstable valley sides.

visible from the viewpoint on the main road near Leighton. Here the patterns of erosion, gravel banks and scroll bars well illustrate their gradual development as they move downstream. At one time or another, therefore, the river has occupied most of the valley floor, thereby removing so much of the glacial deposits that once filled this upper part of the gorge.

Banks of fine, mobile gravel are important to the mechanism of meandering, but the Severn has inherited such a shallow gradient from its glacial origins that the gravels are not moved very much. In many areas the river channel, as any fisherman knows, consists of alternating deep pools - where pike may lurk - and shallow gravely riffles, home of dace and barbel. Historically these riffles have been important as sites for river crossings and fish weirs. They tend to occur at three different types of location. When the river erodes a steep cliff of glacial deposits it can remove the finer sand but leave heavier stones behind that partially fill the channel. Alternatively, existing undulating gravel banks long covered by floodplain silts are simply exposed by the present river - especially at a cross-over point on a valley meander. Thirdly, a tributary can wash more gravel into the river than can be cleared away. At Shrewsbury all three are represented - at Coton Hill, the Welsh Bridge, and the English Bridge respectively.

Just upstream of the English Bridge the Rea Brook enters the Severn and the gravel banks it helped cause in the main channel have induced a 'braided' pattern of channels and islands with a long history of changes. In the thirteenth century the Abbot and town authorities argued about possession of new islands in the stream but they had changed beyond all recognition by the time of sixteenth century maps. The much decayed island still visible downstream of the bridge is of more recent origins, connected with

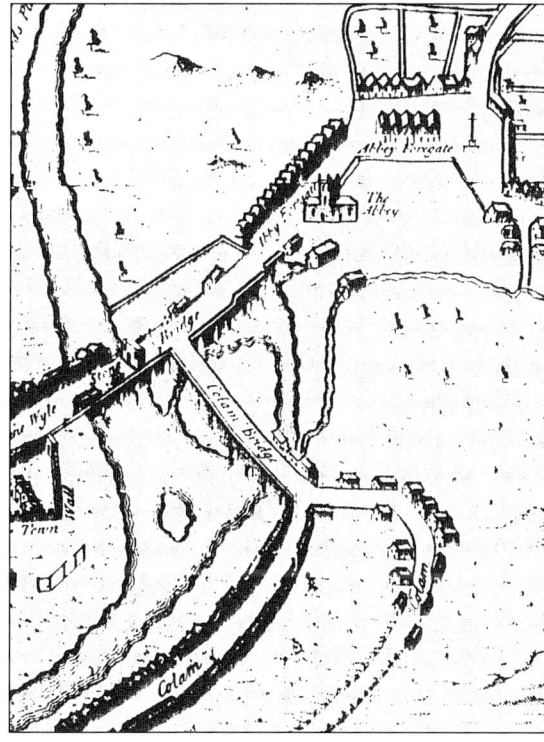

The braiding of the river by the English Bridge shows up well on this 1610 map by John Speed

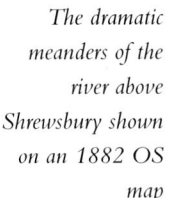

The dramatic meanders of the river above Shrewsbury shown on an 1882 OS map

The bends between Montford Bridge and Shrewsbury are fossilised meanders, inherited from the later glacial meltwater river, and which the present river must blindly follow because they are so deeply incised. There is even more restriction in the Ironbridge Gorge, where the river has to run fairly straight. Around Melverley the thick clay and absence of gravel actually suppresses normal meander development, or at least slows it down.

All this leaves only the reaches around Alberbury, around the mouth of the Tern near Atcham, and between Cressage and Buildwas. Those last meanders are particularly well known, being easily

In general, the historical evidence of the fish weirs and river crossings confirm that the river channel has been remarkably stable for centuries, thanks to its low gradient, the restriction of its incised valley and thick silt. The climate has also been more or less the same since the last Ice Age.

The actual capacity of any river channel, whether deep and narrow or wide and shallow, usually reflects the average size of the floods that it must accommodate once or twice a year. Because of the impervious nature of the Welsh mountains, where the rain runs off quite quickly, the Severn floods also tend to come and go rather quickly. The river channel therefore is only full for a small proportion of the year. Then it can flow past Shrewsbury at a rate of two hundred cubic metres per second. Rare floods spill over the floodplain but seldom linger. For most of the time the water level is well within the banks and for much of the summer the gravel banks and fords are visible.

Over the centuries man has tried to adapt the Severn to his own needs and made his own mark on some aspects of it. Such is the nature of any river system that changes to tributaries also affect the main river. Changes to minor rivers like the Perry and Tern to power water mills or to help drain new farmland have had a direct effect on the Severn itself. Despite all of this, the river still retains many of its natural characteristics - at least in Shropshire - and in a world of so much dredging, embanking, damming and straightening, the Severn is a rare river to study and to enjoy.

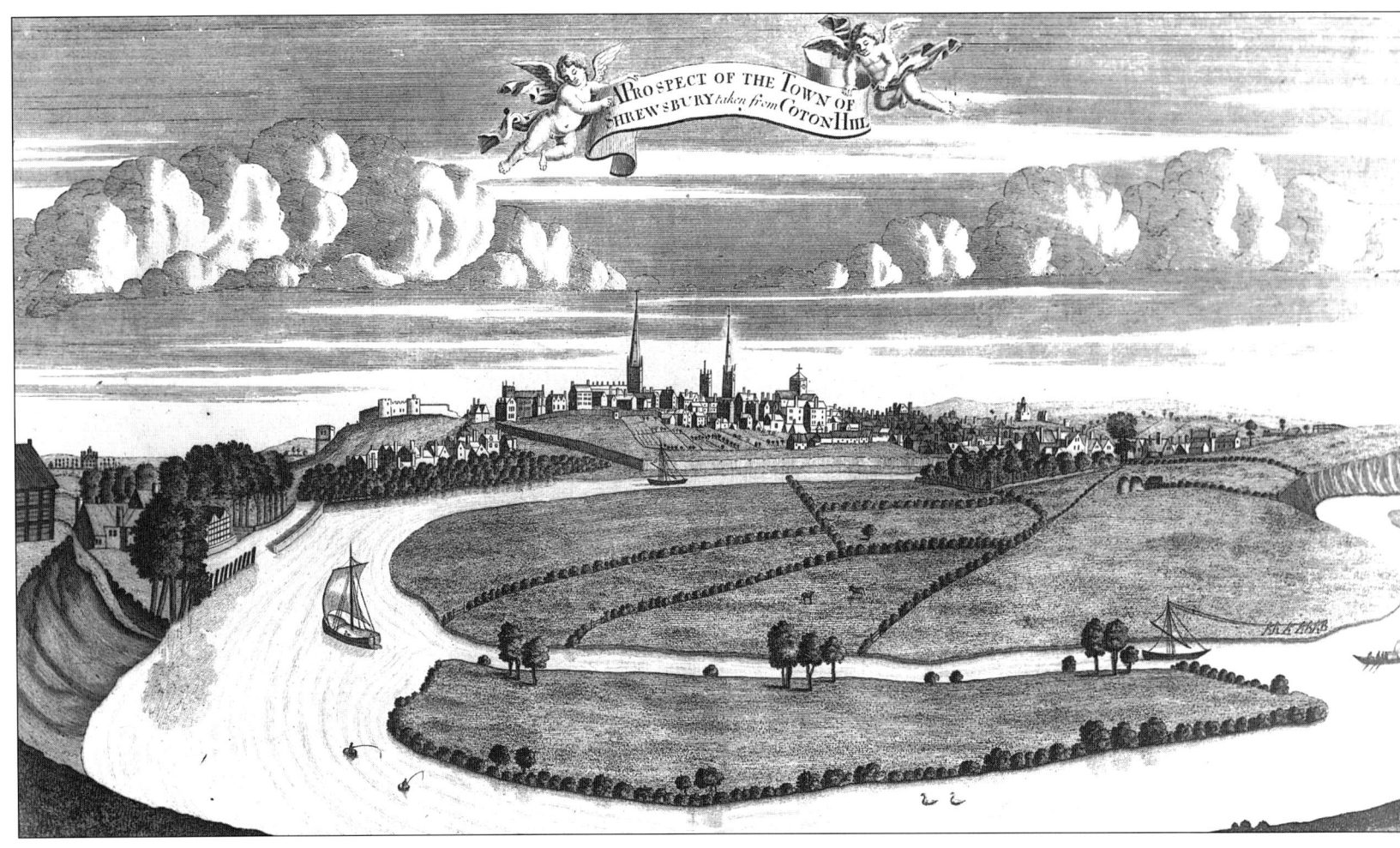

Shrewsbury

Its here the fine river Severn Encompasses ye greatest part of ye town and twines and twists itself about, its not very broad here but is very deep and is Esteemed ye finest river in England to Carry such a depth of water for 80 or more miles together Ere it runns into ye sea which is Bristol.

From 'The Journey of Celia Fiennes' 1698

The Medieval River

For thousands of years the Severn has played an important part in Shropshire's history, but we know relatively little of what went on before the Roman conquest. Here, Dr Paul Stamper takes up the story of the medieval river and explains some of the various ways in which it affected the county.

Throughout the Middle Ages Shropshire was divided into two by the river Severn. Before the county was created in the tenth century, the river formed a natural boundary between kingdoms - of the Magonsaeta to the south and the Wroecensaeta to the north. It also divided the diocese of Hereford to the south from those of St. Asaph and of Lichfield to the north. The latter division is still partly preserved to this day.

The river had a natural military significance, emphasised in the first century AD by the riverside location of the Roman city of Wroxeter - a fort before it became a city. It stood by a ford, by which the main Roman road along the Welsh border crossed the river, and may once have had a bridge. In the centuries following the collapse of the Roman Empire control over such river crossings remained important and were even more so in the ninth century as the master seafarers of the Scandinavian races - the Vikings - began first to raid and then to settle. Shropshire, deep inland, remained largely immune until 895-6 when a great Danish army built a fort and overwintered close to the ford where Bridgnorth would soon develop.

What, in fact, may have been the spur to Bridgnorth's development was the choice fifteen years later by Alfred the Great's daughter Aetheflaeda, ruler of Mercia, of the bluff outcrop above the ford as the site for one of the royal fortified towns called burhs by which control of England was being regained from the Scandinavians. Probably at the same time, and for similar reasons, Shrewsbury, long a royal and ecclesiastical centre, was also chosen to be a burh. It too occupied a

Bridgnorth was an important medieval town and river port, occupying a natural defensive site

good, naturally defensive site and was provided with fortifications and made the administrative centre of one of the new *scires* by which Saxon England was to be governed.

When the Normans arrived in Shropshire in the wake of their victory at Hastings in 1066, it was at Shrewsbury and another crossing point on the Severn - Quatford near Bridgnorth - that two of their principal castles were founded to guard the fords. Quite what form these crossings took, or when bridges first replaced the fords, is not always clear. Of course some crossing places, like that at Shrawardine, again guarded by a castle, never did get bridged. At Bridgnorth, at least, the evidence is clear. There was a bridge there, or close by, when the Danes had camped there in 895-6, presumably made of timber. By the early fourteenth century the bridge (which, like Shrewsbury's, lay on the great road from Chester to Bristol) was in the same place as it is today. In 1322 it was broken down by the Mortimers, then in revolt against Edward the Second. It was probably after

The valley of Bridgnorth

Bridgnorth Bridge, painted in the late eighteenth century by Paul Sandby

that episode that the bridge was rebuilt in stone and in 1478 it was recorded as having eight arches. The importance of the bridge is shown by the fact that well into the Middle Ages the town was known simply as *Bridge*, latinised as *Bruggia* or its shortened form, *Brug*. In fact, as late as the eighteenth century local villagers are said to have still called the town *Bridge*.

Quite when bridges replaced the two natural fords that the Saxon burh of Shrewsbury controlled is unknown. In around 1080 the Normans founded an abbey on the opposite side of the river to the east of the town and if there was not already a bridge in existence to link the two by then it would seem likely that one would soon have been high on the agenda. When finished, this took the traffic on the main road to the Midlands and the south. By the later Middle Ages it consisted of two parts. The main bridge consisted of five stone arches over the main channel of the river, with a further twelve timber-decked spans on stone piers carrying the road clear of the flood level and up into Abbey Foregate. At the end of the bridge was a massive gate tower, with its own drawbridge and prison. By the sixteenth century houses and shops had been built on the bridge. Sometimes called the Stone Bridge, it was also called the English Bridge - to distinguish it from the Welsh Bridge that replaced the other ford carrying the main road west across the river. The medieval Welsh Bridge, which lay at the bottom of Mardol, was similar, with its own great gate tower and, near the middle where there was once a public privy, a row of shops.

In contrast to those bridges in the two main Shropshire towns on the medieval river, the origins of Atcham bridge are fully documented. This is because a case was heard at the Assize of 1221 arising from a complaint by the burgesses of Shrewsbury. They claimed that the Abbot of Lilleshall, who owned the manor of Atcham, had introduced a new charge of a penny on every loaded cart that crossed the bridge. In reply, the Abbot said that in his predecessor's time there had been no bridge at all and the abbey had operated two ferry boats instead which brought in two marks (about £1.33) a year. It had then been decided by a council of William Fitz Alan and other important men that the Abbot should construct a bridge and charge a penny toll for every loaded cart coming from

Gwynne's English Bridge was just finished when this view was painted in 1770. In the background the medieval bridge is being pulled down

The Shropshire Severn

of hindering barge traffic at Bridgnorth. In 1422 the fish weir at Preston Boats near Shrewsbury was said to be obstructing river traffic – although in this case a court upheld the right of the weir to exist because of its ancient origins. Eventually, in 1425, commissioners were appointed to undertake a comprehensive inspection of the banks of the Severn and to pull down any weirs or mills that were obstructing it. By then, the great age of the fish weirs was probably drawing to a close anyway, with many weirs in decline. That at Coton Hill in Shrewsbury, for example, was last recorded in 1531. While there were still twenty-eight in 1575 one or two survived into the reign of Victoria.

Mills and weirs were not the only encroachments along the Severn. In 1272 the Greyfriars at Bridgnorth were accused of taking *'stones and other rubbish from the banks of the Severn, and throwing them into the river, whereby they have realised to themselves a piece of ground 150 feet long by 50 feet wide, and this they have enclosed. By which process the [artificial] bank causes the water to pound upon the king's mills, and this was done sixteen years back.'* Much later, one of the first pieces of evidence for the intensification of coal mining in the Ironbridge Gorge area is a complaint made in 1575 to the Commissioners of Sewers. This was a body set up to ensure that inland waterways remained navigable. They were told of the nuisance caused by the tipping of mining spoil into the Severn at the Tuckies, near Broseley. With the arrival of industrial pollution, the story of the River Severn suddenly, and sadly, becomes more familiar to modern readers.

The Buck brothers' view of Bridgnorth in the early eighteenth century

site. Many fish bones were found, most being marine species including ling, cod, hake, conger and herring. A small number of river and freshwater fish bones were also found, such as eel, pike, and roach – and it is likely that some, at least, of these came from the Severn. Not all would have been caught in weirs. In 1309 a fisherman was taxed on his boat and nets at Shrewsbury, and the abbey, which had large fish or stew ponds to the south (now under the car-park) probably employed its own fisherman to supply the heavy demands for fish on Fridays and feast days.

Despite the barge gutters, weirs clearly would interfere with the barge traffic on the Severn, and from the thirteenth century onwards complaints about the nuisance caused by these 'kiddles' are regularly recorded. In 1268 Henry of Ribbeford was appointed to find out who was responsible for narrowing and raising weirs on the Severn between Gloucester and Shrewsbury. Encroachments were apparently still common much later. For instance in 1415 the Abbot of Lilleshall was accused

A similar concern for access to both customers and to water can be seen elsewhere in the plan of medieval Shrewsbury - in Dogpole, for instance. Towards the bottom of Mardol the plots curve sharply towards the river. The reason here may also have been to give some of the more noxious trades - such as tanners and dyers - ready access to the vast quantities of water that they required. In fact by about 1300 almost all tanners and a good number of the dyers were concentrated close to the river in the industrial suburb of Frankwell, which must have been a foul and odoriferous place to live or work.

Despite the pollution from such industries the river was far cleaner than it later became and abounded in one of the medieval staple foods - fish. In 1086, when the Domesday Book was compiled, there were at least eighteen separate fisheries on the county's rivers. Most were on the peaty rivers of the north - the Perry, Tern, Roden and their tributaries - and from these vast numbers of eels were taken each year. On the Severn itself there were at least seven fisheries by the end of the Middle Ages and salmon may have been more important. The basic techniques of catching the fish were the same, relying on fish traps and nets suspended from timber-framed weirs built across shallow parts of the river. To allow boats, and a proportion of fish, to pass the weir unhindered, a by-pass channel was built around it. This created a typically long, thin island - or bylet - in the river with the channel - sometimes called a barge gutter - on one side and the weir on the other.

Each weir was usually worked by a tenant who lived nearby and who could combine tending the fish traps with working a small-holding, operating a ferry, or tending a withy-bed - growing willows for basket-making and the like. A weir could be a very valuable and much sought after asset. Monastic houses, in particular, seemed to have been keen to acquire fisheries. In the thirteenth century the Abbot of Lilleshall built a fishery between Atcham and Cronkhill on a stretch of river granted to him by Shrewsbury Abbey. Presumably for the same reasons, Shrewsbury Abbey purchased a narrow strip of land three hundred yards long in Castlefields, downstream of their abbey on the opposite bank from their own land in Abbey Foregate. The site of their fish weir is still marked by a bylet and barge gutter.

All along the river there are similar survivals in various stages of completeness but other than these the remaining evidence of the Severn fisheries is very limited. Some ideas on the fish being eaten in medieval Shropshire have come to light recently in excavations on the Shrewsbury Abbey

A barge at Shrewsbury being bow-hauled, a detail from the Burghley map

untamed natural river, and the barge gutters around the fish weirs, restricted the size of boat that could be used. For traffic going long distances, Shrewsbury merchants presumable transhipped their cargoes into larger craft at a port further downstream - probably Bristol. Certainly that was the practice of the Gloucester merchants. Barges are occasionally mentioned in medieval records, as are trows. In 1411 the townsmen of Gloucester and Bristol joined together in a complaint that they were being forced to pay extortionate hire fees for trows belonging to the men of Bewdley (Worcestershire), Shropshire, and Wales to carry their goods on the upper part of the Severn. How closely these vessels resembled their eighteenth, and nineteenth, century namesakes is unknown. A trow is shown on the famous Burghley map of late-sixteenth century Shrewsbury being hauled by four men on the bank.

Far more mundane, perhaps, though no less important, was the role of the river in towns such as Bridgnorth and Shrewsbury. It provided most of the water for drinking and washing and also took away the sewage. In the late Saxon and Norman town some of the main properties in Shrewsbury were quite narrow but very long, running back from a frontage on Pride Hill right down to the river. Almost certainly this was to give the merchants not only a frontage on one of the main trading thoroughfares but also direct and private access to the Severn, where some may have had private wharves. An incidental benefit may well have been lush grazing on the riverside land for any animals, such as a horse, that the merchant may have had.

The Medieval River

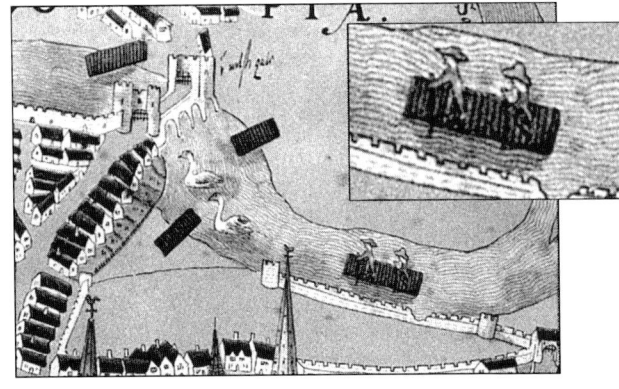

A flotte - a raft of timber - taken from the sixteenth century Burghley map

Shrewsbury when £3 worth of wood got trapped in the town weir at Coton. The large flottes could equally be a hazard in their own right, especially when the floatmen 'shot' the rafts under the bridge arches - a practice banned, in theory, in 1536. It obviously continued, and in March 1579 a float smashed into, and dislodged, a prop supporting some old overhanging shops on the English Bridge at Shrewsbury. They collapsed and fell into the river, taking with them a butcher's four-year-old daughter who, incredibly, managed to survive.

Amongst the wares being transported up the river into the county in the early Middle Ages was wine from the vineyards of Gascony, then an English possession. This was an expensive commodity, destined principally for the tables of the nobility and the wealthy. From time to time the Sheriff, the King's representative in the county, was required to purchase wine in Bristol and to arrange its carriage to places in Shropshire to be ready for a royal visit. In the twelfth and thirteenth centuries the king came to the county fairly regularly. For example, King John visited five times between 1200 and 1216, and Henry the Third at least nine times between 1221 and 1267. In preparation for Henry's 1245 visit the Sheriff was ordered to arrange a fairly small consignment of twenty tuns of wine. A tun was a wooden barrel containing 252 gallons. He was to leave eight tuns at Shrewsbury, and four each at Much Wenlock, Bridgnorth and Bobbington, Staffordshire. Other customers included the wealthier clergy. In 1281 the rector of Pattingham, just over the Staffordshire border, bought a tun of wine at Bridgnorth. Some of the rougher sort of wine did find its way into taverns.

Another luxury product from mainland Europe being shipped upstream was olive oil and in 1411, along with wine and other goods, this was liable for toll at Bridgnorth. At the end of the Middle Ages the list of goods reaching Shropshire by river included wine, alum (for fixing dyes and preparing skins), pig iron, teasel staffs, and malt.

Relatively little is known about the vessels used to carry all these cargoes. Both shallows on the and the scene of several parleys between the often warring Welsh and English. In the dispute it was said that anyone crossing the bridge paid tolls to John de Hagerwas. These he retained, according to an agreement with the Crown, on condition that he kept the bridge in good repair. Hagerwas was about to fulfil his side of the bargain when he died. The Abbot of Haughmond and John Sprenchose, appointed to audit his accounts, noted that while his receipts had been £19 8s. 1d. he had spent over £36 on dressed stone and timber that was stored at his house ready to be used in the repairs.

This was a variety of a grant by the Crown of pontage - the right to devote the income from tolls charged to repair the bridge. Such a grant was made to the borough of Bridgnorth in the early 1330's and to the Abbot of Buildwas to facilitate the repair of Buildwas bridge in 1354. Later it seems to have been recognised as an act of piety to leave money for bridge repair in wills. At Bridgnorth William Boblar left 12d. in 1438 and Gillian Walton, widow, 5s. in 1501 for just that purpose.

Whilst perhaps not all were conscious of the fact, the Severn was the principal link between Shropshire and the outside world. In the Middle Ages it was navigable as far upstream as Pool Quay, over the Welsh border in Montgomeryshire. A stone weir at Strata Marcella Abbey held up water to supply mill leats and barred further progress.

At least some of the wool and cloth produced in Shropshire must have been exported down river and on to Europe. In the thirteenth century the monks of Buildwas secured the right to load their wool on to barges at Cressage. At Gloucester corn from the surrounding area was exported in considerable quantities and the same was probably true of other major ports on the river, including Shrewsbury. By the sixteenth century skins, leather, ale, dairy produce and honey were also regularly shipped downstream, and there is no reason to think that these were in any way new cargoes at that time. Coal was being carried down the Severn in barges from Benthall and other places at least by the 1320's. Timber, too, was taken down river, lashed together raft fashion in float woods or *flottes*. In the fifteenth century firewood was being supplied to both Gloucester and Bristol.

The flottes, large and difficult to control, were clearly a problem - made worse by the practice of lashing the timbers together at places as far upstream as Alberbury and holding them there until the river was well 'up' and able to carry them rapidly down river. Float wood seems often to have become caught up in the many fish weirs. Around 1520 six Welsh floatmen sought redress from

The massive gate-tower of the medieval Welsh Bridge, painted by the Revd. Hugh Owen in 1823

Shrewsbury and a half-penny for all other carts. That bridge, at the time of the Assize, was only one arch away from completion – so all the evidence suggests that the bridge was begun by Abbot Ralph sometime between 1210 and 1220, and finished in, or shortly after, 1221, by Abbot Alan.

Usually, details of how the bridges were built, financed and maintained are sketchy. Even where there are records of a dispute over repairs – as in the 1292 Assize when Montford bridge was reported as being broken down – only little snippets are revealed to show how the bridges were managed. The bridge at Montford would have been well known at the time, being on the main road north

The Medieval River

Coalbrookdale wants nothing but Cerberus to give you an idea of the
heathen hell. The Severn may pass for the Styx, with this difference
that Charon, turned turnpike man, ushers you over the bridge instead of
rowing in his crazy boat;

Extract from Charles Dibdin 1801-2

'Coalbrookdale by night'
P. J. de Loutherbourg 1801

The Navigation

In the medieval period the river's role as a major transport artery, at a time when roads were few and far between, had been enshrined by laws freeing the `King's high stream of Severn' from tolls. In this section Dr. Barrie Trinder, the Senior Research Fellow at the Ironbridge Institute, shows how the navigation continued to grow in importance from the Elizabethan time onwards, stimulating and sustaining Shropshire's Industrial Revolution in the eighteenth century.

The Severn was the source of much of Shropshire's prosperity by the end of the reign of Elizabeth the first and remained so for nearly three centuries. Richard Brooke of Madeley, who died in 1670, owned a vessel called the *Jonathan* worth £40. Abel Jones of Shrewsbury, who died in the same year, had a pair of barges worth £42, and Francis Ap Owen of Dowles, who died the year before, had a trow, a barge and a boat worth £100 - as well as wood to the same value awaiting shipment on the Severn. These were all rich men by the standards of the time, but the value of all the movable possessions of another riverman, Edward Dawley of Broseley Wood, in 1670 was only just over £12, and his barge worth less than £9. The contrast highlights the two main types of traffic on the Severn.

The wealthier owners were concerned with the long-distance carriage to ports below Gloucester, particularly Bristol, of Shropshire's more valuable exports - iron, leather, grain, cheese and paper - and with the return cargoes of tobacco, wine, spirits, Baltic timber and most other goods that could not be produced within the county. At least some of their vessels needed to be capable of navigating the dangerous tidal waters of the Severn below Gloucester.

Many bargemen - perhaps the majority - never sailed so far but made their living by carrying bulk cargoes over short distances, particularly taking coal from the Ironbridge Gorge downstream to Bridgnorth, Bewdley, Worcester and Gloucester.

A barge near Buildwas, captured in watercolour by the Rev. Williams in the late eighteenth century

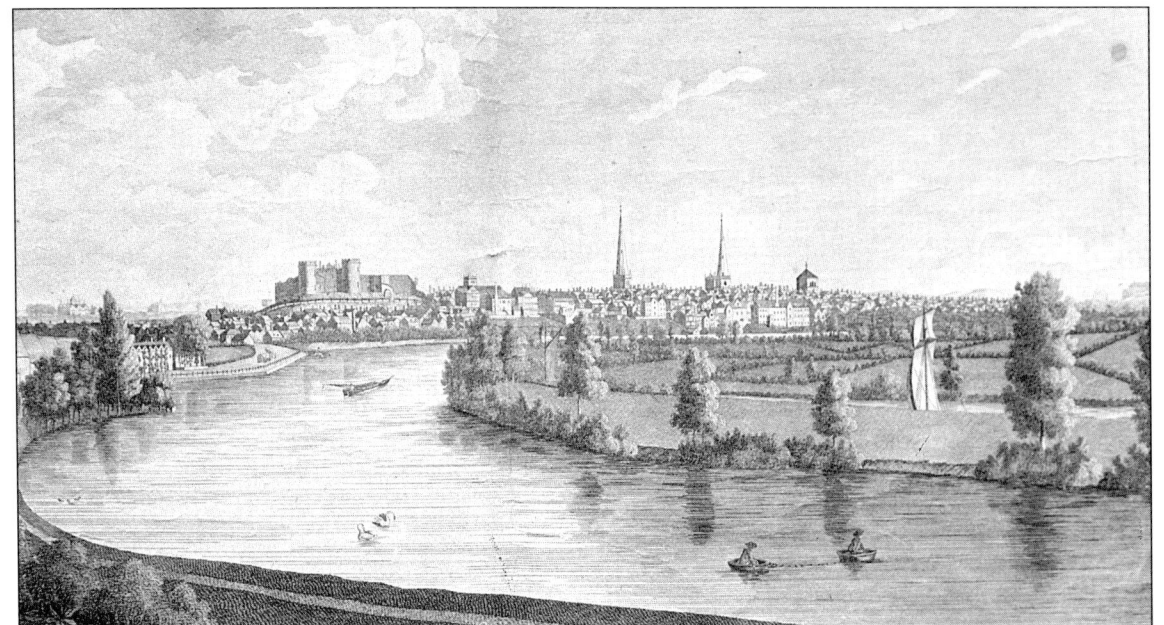

This eighteenth century engraving by Sanders of Shrewsbury is full of interest. In the foreground a pair of coraclers net for fish; beyond, a barge negotiates the barge gutter, and another has its mast lowered

The analysis of the Port Books of Gloucester at the University of Wolverhampton has shown that the Severn navigation formed part of a thriving commercial economy by 1700. It made possible the growth of the Shropshire iron industry in the eighteenth century. In conjunction with the Staffordshire & Worcestershire Canal (which joined the river at Stourport), it carried the produce of the Shropshire ironworks to numerous customers in the Black country and Birmingham. After the completion in 1794 of the Shropshire Canal from Donnington Wood to Coalport, it was able to carry increasing quantities of coal down river - about 50,000 tons a year being exported from Coalport alone by around 1800, and as much as 80,000 tons by 1830.

The Shropshire portion of the Severn was never 'improved'. In 1786 a bill to permit the construction of sixteen locks between Worcester and Coalbrookdale was rejected by the House of Commons. The scheme's engineer was William Jessop, the most able canal engineer of the time, but it was defeated because of opposition from, amongst others, the Shropshire bargemen. The local historian John Randall remarked some eighty years later that *"As a class bargeowners are opposed to innovation"*, and that the oldest men remembered how, when George the Third was king, they had shouted themselves hoarse and tossed their caps in the air in honour of victory over these attempts to improve the channel.

When the river below Stourport was improved by the construction of locks in the 1840's, the Shropshire bargeowners were given exemption from tolls, but there was no serious proposal to build locks further upstream. As late as 1892 another scheme proposed to canalise the river by building nine locks between Stourport and Buildwas. Neither it, nor any other late-Victorian proposals, came anywhere near realisation.

The Shropshire Severn thus remained a river which could be used without payment, and which was free from the kind of bureaucratic control that generates minute books and accounts. Our understanding of the navigation has to be built up from a variety of other sources, not all directly related to the river, including probate records, census returns, newspapers, the accounts of customers of the navigation, pictures of the ships and river ports at work, and the archaeology which remains on the banks.

The last English Bridge in the early 1900's, showing its distinctive hump and the wider 'navigation arch' in the centre

The Navigation

The trow William - one of the last to work the river - at Jackfield

In 1758 a Coalbrookdale man, George Perry, wrote a description of vessels on the Severn and distinguished *trows* - of between 40 and 80 tons with main, top, and sometimes mizzen masts - from single-masted *barges or frigates* - of between 20 and 40 tons. Both types could be up to 60 feet long. Such a classification can be confusing, but Perry was probably trying to show the difference between larger vessels which could safely navigate the estuary and those which usually went no further downstream than Gloucester.

Among the most valuable vessels recorded in the eighteenth century were the 'great trow at Gloucester' owned by Francis Owen of Madeley in 1732 and worth £70; his 'middle trow' valued at £60; a trow belonging to Richard Lacon of Bridgnorth valued at over £67 in 1735; and the trow *Loving Brother* owned by Thomas Andrews of Bridgnorth in 1723 worth £60. These vessels were intended for trade in the Bristol Channel, to the ports of South Wales, and on the Stroudwater Navigation.

Vessels which could travel on below Gloucester were in the minority amongst those operated by Shropshire owners. Most barges were smaller and less valuable. While vessels from the county traded down to Bristol well into the nineteenth century, an increasing amount of traffic after 1700 seems to have been transhipped to larger trows at Gloucester.

Many owners had ranges of vessels like the Shrewsbury owner whose fleet in 1812 consisted of the 40 ton *Defiance,* the 35 ton *Mary*, and the 14 ton *William*. John Rees, also of Shrewsbury, was working until 1835 with two barges, the 55 ton *Cambrian* and the 42 ton *Hannah*, as well as a boat of 7 tons. The twenty boats working from Shrewsbury in 1835 ranged from a 6 ton boat to a pair of 50 ton barges. One of these larger vessels, Thomas Bratton's *Eliza*, was sketched whilst moored at the town's Frankwell Quay by William Vandyck Brown. Lists of vessels often include 'boats'. These were small vessels, little more than sizable rowing boats, which appear on illustrations of Shrewsbury and Bridgnorth. They were probably used to move goods between barges and wharves.

The larger vessels worked with crews of up to four men. Two vessels were moored overnight at Madeley on Census night in 1861 - the *Hannah*, on which there were three watermen, and the *Industry*, where slept the captain, Thomas Doughty, and three watermen.

Whatever their size, most Severn vessels were of similar construction. They were clinker-built -

The end. Remnants of a trow lie close to the site of Shrewsbury weir at around the turn of the century

that is their planks were not laid flush onto the framing but overlapped. They had 'D-shaped' sterns and masts that could be lowered to pass under bridges. Contemporary inventories or lists of goods provide evidence of some of the equipment carried on board - from chains, ropes and tarpaulins to windlasses and anchors. Some had awnings that could be erected over the stern sections to provide accommodation for the crew in want of a cabin.

The first iron boat, John Wilkinson's celebrated *Trial*, was launched on the Severn at Willey Wharf in 1788. Although it and its sister craft proved no cheaper than boats of conventional timber construction, iron vessels were not unusual on the river in the nineteenth century. The Onions family of ironmasters were working four iron barges in 1820, one worth as much as £150. The wrought-iron frigate *Salop* was offered for sale at Meadow Wharf, Coalbrookdale, in 1837 and in 1843 a lugger, with a semi-cylindrical hull was built at Ironbridge.

The Navigation

In the eighteenth century barges were constructed in Shrewsbury on the site now occupied by the Sixth Form College downstream of the Welsh Bridge. They were also built at the Bower Yard, Benthall, at several sites in and around Jackfield, at the Rovings a little further downstream, and in three yards in Bridgnorth. By 1851 only two barge builders remained, Edward Gething at the Bower Yard and William Oakes at Bridgnorth.

The Shropshire Severn was always a natural river and its water level thus varied considerably. For long periods there was insufficient water for navigation at all, which meant that much of a bargeman's time was spent waiting. The principal trade, in coal from the Ironbridge Gorge, was dependent on 'flushes' - sudden increases in the water level. In 1784 it was said that when the level rose it was common for between sixty and eighty vessels to leave the Gorge at once, carrying as much as

Boatbuilding at the Bower Yard, Ironbridge, in the middle of the last century

4,000 tons of coal downstream. In May 1836 Charles Hulbert counted no less than 72 craft from Coalport Bridge. Even as late as 1882, advantage was taken of a sudden flush to move large stocks of brick and tile from wharfes in the Gorge to customers at Worcester and Gloucester.

John Randall wrote in the 1850's that Shropshire barges *'go down with the stream and are drawn back by horses'*. Bargemen also made use of sails, when and where this was possible. In good water the journey from Ironbridge to Gloucester took about twenty-four hours, but few vessels were able to accomplish more than twenty return voyages a year.

There were once many ferries across the river. Coalport Ferry was replaced by the Memorial Bridge in the early 1920's

Before the construction of proper horse towpaths, vessels were dragged upstream by gangs of 'bow haulers', who were the subject of much moral disapproval from the propertied classes along the river. Some of the smaller boats often seen in river views may have been used to ferry home bow haulers after they had dragged a vessel up over the section they were accustomed to work. To observe the circuitous course of the Severn upstream from Shrewsbury, between low sandy cliffs, shows that bow haulers must have spent much of their time wading through the water.

Towpaths enabled horses to take over the work of the bow haulers. The path between Bewdley and Coalbrookdale was authorised in 1772 but was not completed until 1800. The path from Coalbrookdale to Frankwell Quay, Shrewsbury, received parliamnetary assent in May 1809 and was completed by the following November. No towpath was constructed upstream from Frankwell, although some traffic continued to use this stretch of the river until the end of the century. No records of the towpath companies survive, but there is some archaeological evidence of their activities.

The Navigation

The towpath acts designated one side or other of the river as the right of way. From Shrewsbury it was the left bank, going downstream, then the right bank from the horse ferry provided by the company at Underdale as far as Cressage Bridge. From there it followed the left bank to Coalport, and thence the right bank past the county boundary to Bewdley. Bridges were provided across most of the tributaries at their points of confluence. An iron bridge cast by the Coalbrookdale Company in 1828 crosses the mouth of the Borle Brook, whilst the Mor Brook is spanned by one cast by Onions of Broseley in 1824. A small stone arched bridge crosses the mouth of the Leighton Brook.

A Victorian transport interchange - plateways meet trows at Loadcroft Wharf

This cast-iron bridge of 1828 was made by the Coalbrookdale Company to take the new horse tow-path across the Borle Brook

There is no trace of any bridge across the mouth of the Cound Brook.

Between Eardington and Arley evidence can be observed of excavation to create a more level course for the towpath. Erosion has revealed that this section was resurfaced from time to time, on some occasions with waste materials from the Coalport Chinaworks. The towpaths were financed by tolls charged on horses - not on boats - and the companies were responsible for clearing fords for the passage of vessels at low water.

The principal concentrations of barge owners and crews were in the Ironbridge Gorge and Bridgnorth. There was also a community in Shrewsbury, consistently of five or six owners each with several craft, from the 1630 to the 1830's. Owners also lived at some smaller settlements along the river at which were wharves for loading and unloading cargoes. There was a 'common landing place for timber' near the mouth of the River Perry in 1728, and a quay at Pimley with a warehouse where iron was landed in the 1660's. Cound Lane End was a wharf of some importance, and the home of the Dodson family who had a fleet of barges. There was a mooring at Cressage, from which a barge broke loose in 1791, crashing into the temporary bridge at Buildwas, and a wharf at Sheinton where a man drowned in 1862. At the Rovings in Barrow parish were situated a boat building yard, a wharf where Caughley porcelain was loaded, and a public house - traditionally kept by a bargeowner and closed by the 1860's. Further downstream there was a small wharf at Bargate in Kinlet parish, and at the extremity of the county at Dowles, a 'load' for the dispatch of timber from the Wyre Forest area was in use by the eighteenth century.

Some of the Severn's tributaries were also navigable. The lower reaches of the Vyrnwy were certainly used by barges carrying iron and lead ore in the early eighteenth century, and in 1824 one Thomas Jones of Melverley stole a cow's hide from a barge on that river. The Tern also carried barges. A vessel sunk in the river near Attingham Park in 1757 had once been used by Joshua Gee the ironmaster to convey iron to Upton Forge, and Coalbrookdale Company accounts record the dispatch by river of small quantities of pig iron to Tern Forge in 1737-8. The best evidence for this navigation is archaeological. In 1969 Dr. Michael Lewis excavated the remains of a lock at the

The river near Cressage with the Wrekin in the background

River craft moored by Bridgnorth bridge in 1776 - an engraving by R. Godfrey

mouth of the river which had walls of ashlar blocks joined by iron cramps set in lead, and a floor of transverse timbers with brick paving. It could have taken a boat 23 feet long and 7 feet 8 inches wide (7m by 2.33m) and was probably built around 1710 when Tern Forge was being constructed. In about 1797 Humphrey Repton, the landscape gardener, cut away one side and incorporated it into a weir designed to create a lake visible from Attingham Park. The weir collapsed in a flood in the 1830's.

The Shropshire portion of the Severn Navigation declined during the nineteenth century and commercial traffic ceased before the century's end. The Montgomeryshire Canal took away much of the traffic from the upper part of the river above Shrewsbury but timber and stone were still being carried in the 1850's. The demise of traffic between Shrewsbury and Coalbrookdale is shown by the decline in the numbers of owners and watermen recorded by census. In Shrewsbury, it fell from 18 in 1841 to three in 1851, although at least one Shrewsbury boat was operating in the 1860's.

One vessel helped to bring about the demise of the navigation. The *Christiana*, launched near Coleham Bridge in Shrewsbury in September 1858, was a twin-engined steam-powered paddle tug which hauled barges of materials for the construction of the Severn Valley Railway. That railway took away much of the traffic downstream from Ironbridge previously carried by river. The last regular traffic in pig iron ceased in 1869, by which time very little coal was being carried. Limestone traffic in the Ironbridge Gorge ceased in 1878. The most regular remaining freight was in bricks and roofing tiles from Jackfield. There were only 36 barges and 9 boats left on the Shropshire portion of the river in 1869, and many of them were offered for sale in the next two decades. Only about a dozen watermen were listed in the Ironbridge Gorge in the 1881 census. A barge carrying firebricks from the Gorge sank after it hit one of the piers of Bridgnorth bridge during the afternoon of the 25th January 1895. The sinking marked the end of the commercial navigation of the Shropshire Severn.

To Buildwas Bridge by Severnside

So long ago and yet it seems but yesterday!
The three of us would wend our way
Through Coalbrookdale to Severnside,
Where here and there a boat would glide
To lend enchantment to the scene.

Here we would pause and dream,
Then take the narrow path that leads
Along the bank where dragonflies - like small mosaic pieces,
In mid-air-softly dart.

By the fringed path we wandered
Nor turned aside until we reached
The Buildwas bridge and road to Wenlock town;
Up hill then down along a peaceful country road
Where tranquil brooklet flows all bordered by a grey stone wall.

Here - loveliest sight of all -
A wide green verge on either side
Lay thick with violets, blue and white,
Whose colour far outvies the pale forget-me-not.

Untroubled by the sound of wheels
All heedless of the time that steals
Upon us in this dear familiar place,
We find that we must mend our pace.

See, darkling clouds foretell the rain
And we must catch the Severn Valley train.

1962 *Gwen Simmonds*

BRIDGES OVER THE SHROPSHIRE SEVERN

As well as being an important transport highway, the river also acted as a barrier to other forms of travelling. As recently as the middle of the eighteenth century there were bridges across the Severn only at Montford, Shrewsbury, Atcham, Buildwas, and Bridgnorth. Today there are over thirty bridges across the Shropshire Severn, ranging from the medieval to the modern. Those who would like to know more about the county's bridges in general should read the late Anthony Blackwall's 'Historic Bridges of Shropshire' (Shropshire Books 1985), from which much of the following information has been taken.

The earliest river crossings were simply fords, sited where the river was shallow enough to cross and dictating the pattern of the local road system. Apart from a possible Roman bridge at Wroxeter, there appear to have been no bridges across the river at all until the very late Saxon period. Then, at the end of the ninth century, there is reference to one at Cwatbryge - assumed to be either at Quatford or Bridgnorth. The early bridges would have been of timber, possibly with stone footings or piers. Later stone became the main material for the bridges over the river, although timber continued to be used on occassion. For example, Telford built Cressage Bridge in timber at the end of the eighteenth century and, as late as the 1860's, the railway bridge at Melverley was built of wood.

The world-famous iron bridge that gave its name to Ironbridge demonstrated the possibilities of iron in 1779. For the next century, cast-iron was the main building material for major engineering works. Bridge design became more sophisticated - seen for example in Telford's Buildwas Bridge of 1796 that used much less iron and yet was far stronger. Cast iron reached its zenith in the county in the form of the Albert Edward Bridge at Buildwas of 1862. It was gradually replaced by wrought

Belvidere bridge, shortly after it was restored in the early 1980's

iron in the second half of the nineteenth century, for example in Shrewsbury's Greyfriars Bridge (1879). Wrought iron, in turn, was replaced by steel, as in the Port Hill suspension bridge. The twentieth century gave birth to new materials, such as the reinforced concrete used in the recently demolished Jackfield Free Bridge (1909) and the present Cressage Bridge (1913).

Today's bridges over the Shropshire Severn vary in date, design and material. In the following pages, the bridges are listed in downstream order, from the Welsh to Worcestershire borders.

Melverley

The first of the county's bridges, between Melverley and Crew Green, is no architectural masterpiece. There was no bridge at this point linking England and Wales until the ambitious company that eventually became the Potteries, Shrewsbury & North Wales Railway ('The Potts') opened a branch line in the 1860's. The present steel girder bridge is the third on the site, built in 1947-8 with standard military materials. The branch closed for the last time in 1960 and the bridge was due to be demolished. Sensibly, the local councils decided to keep it and convert it to a road bridge - using the track bed on either side to take a new lane from Melverey to Crew Green and providing a much needed crossing. This accounts for the wide sweeping approaches to the bridge from either side. It re-opened in its new role in 1962.

Melverley bridge was built for trains but now takes road traffic instead

Montford Bridge

There are now two bridges at Montford Bridge, an important bridging point since the medieval period. The first is the modern and typically mundane steel and concrete road bridge carrying the heavy traffic on the new A5. The other, despite alterations, has the hallmarks of elegance and craftsmanship so lacking from the cost-conscious Department of Transport. Built in 1792, it replaced a medieval bridge 50 yards downstream. Thomas Telford was then the county surveyor and this

Telford's Montford Bridge and datestone

bridge was his first major project. He used a local partnership, John Carline and John Tilley, to build it. The quality of the sandstone masonry in the three graceful spans - the centre one slightly wider than the others - is superb. The bridge needed repairing in the early 1960's and was widened at the same time with reinforced concrete. Now that the new bridge has been built, perhaps it would be possible for this one to be restored to its original condition. That would have the added benefit of dissuading drivers to continue to use this old part of the A5 as a short cut.

Shrewsbury

Frankwell Footbridge

Although there are threats in the air to build a new road bridge at Shelton, the first bridge the Severn flows under in the county town is the modern footbridge linking Frankwell meadows and the town's Riverside. This is a striking design by Mott, Hay & Anderson, opened in 1979 - basically a suspension bridge with only one pylon, known technically as a cable-stayed suspension bridge. It has a distinct bounce to it, delighting countless children jumping up and down as they cross. Arguably, it is the best of the new bridges across the river.

The Welsh Bridge

The magnificent medieval Welsh Bridge stood a little upstream of the present one, and Mardol ran straight down to it. On the Frankwell side of the river the approaches are still visible tucked away between commercial premises. The five-arched bridge of today was built by the same firm as Montford Bridge, Carline and Tilley, and was opened in 1795. The middle arch is wider than the others and was known to boatmen as the 'navigation arch'. On the west bank is a land-arch across the former tow-path, and in the balustrade there is still the pulley that helped haul barges through the bridge to the wharves upstream. Telford warned that the bridge was in the wrong place because of the scouring by the river. He was soon proved right, and in 1833 a lot of work had to be done to the footings. Nevertheless, the bridge still stands and takes volumes of traffic unthought of in the eighteenth century. Once again, the quality of the masonry is impeccable.

The Welsh Bridge

than those, this is a pity. The bridge was designed by Joseph Locke and Robert Stephenson and officially opened in 1849. Built of brick, with masonry trimmings, it has four arches crossing the river as well as three more on the Abbey Foregate bank. Shrewsbury was a major railway centre and by the end of the nineteenth century the station had become extremely cramped. As a result, it was decided to extend the platforms over the river and to increase the number of tracks. Additional steel girder bridges were built on either side of the first bridge between 1899 and 1902. It has to be said that they are no asset to the riverscape. The regrettable run-down in our railway system has meant less rail traffic and less need for all that track across the Severn. Perhaps now it will be possible to get rid of these steel eye-sores and leave just the original bridge.

Castle Walk Foot Bridge

The present single-span bridge replaced an earlier suspension bridge in 1951. It is an early example of a post-tensioned, pre-stressed concrete bridge - whatever that means - and has a span of about 250 feet. It provides a very useful short-cut for pedestrians between Castlefields and Underdale. There was almost another bridge just downstream, close to where the weir now is. A bridge to carry the main line of the Potteries & Shrewsbury Junction Railway, later a part of the 'Potts' - over the river was started in the mid-1860's but then abandoned.

Telford Way Bridge

The Telford Way Bridge carries the inner ring-road across the river and was opened in 1964. In design, and appearance, it is a bigger version of the Castle Walk Foot Bridge - but with three spans.

Eastern By-pass Bridges

The recent construction of the new A5 extension to the M54, and the link to it from the north by the re-routed A49, has meant three new crossings of the river between Uffington and Emstrey. All are typical Department of Transport fare, scarcely worth a mention.

Belvidere, or Preston Boats, Bridge

In between the second and the third of the by-pass bridges is a reminder of how bridges should be same architect's bridge at Atcham. In the 1920's, modern traffic was finding the bridge restrictive, and it was decided to knock it down and build anew. The local borough engineer, Arthur Ward, persuaded the powers-that-be to try to copy the old design as far as practicable - and to save as much of the old facing stone and decoration as possible as well. This was duly done, and the new stone bridge could easily be mistaken for the old - apart from being wider and with a less pronounced hump. Queen Mary passed over the still unfinished bridge in 1923, and it was later decided, with her permission, to count that as the official opening!

The Railway Bridges

There are really three railway bridges carrying tracks and platforms across the river. The original one is in the middle, and virtually hidden by the later ones. As it is a far better piece of architecture

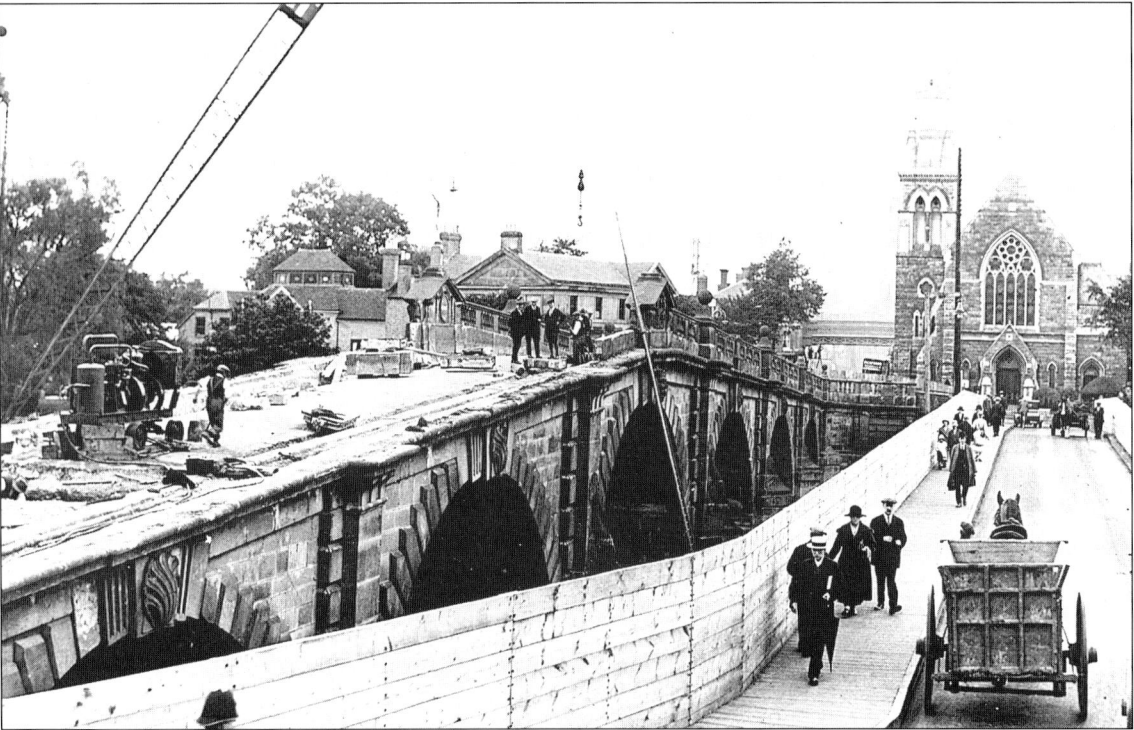

A temporary wooden bridge was needed when the old English Bridge (on the left) was demolished in the early 1920's and then replaced by the present one

The one that finally succeeded was funded and built by a private company, the Kingsland Bridge Company, still in business and still charging a small toll for car and foot passengers - 5p and 1p respectively - and recently upgrading to automatic barriers. They also had to build expensive approach roads on each side and, because of the difference in height of the parts they were connecting, the roadway of the bridge is high above the river. The wrought iron bridge was designed by Thomas Charles Townsend and opened in 1883. It is a 'bow-string' bridge, with the roadway suspended from the single segmental arch, and has a span of 65 metres.

Kingsland Bridge, Shrewsbury

Greyfriars Bridge

This footbridge linking the town with Coleham gets its name from the ruins of the Franciscan Friary nearby. It is a quite prosaic wrought-iron affair built in 1879 by the Cochrane Company of Dudley. Its design is technically a 'hog-backed Pratt truss'!

English Bridge

The present English Bridge was not built in the eighteenth century and later widened, and nor was it re-opened by Queen Mary in 1923 - despite the plaque. These are simply two common traditions that still persist. The medieval bridge was in two parts - one over the Severn itself, the other over the complex of channels on the edge of the Abbey Foregate. In the late 1760's, John Gwynne designed a graceful replacement to the main bridge. Opened in 1774, it had a distinct 'hump' to allow as much rooms as possible in the central navigation arch. In design, it was very similar to the

Porthill Bridge, Shrewsbury

Port Hill Footbridge

Until the late nineteenth century there were no bridges between the Welsh and English ones, people relying on a series of small ferries. There are now three additional bridges, and, despite its design, the Port Hill bridge is the newest of the three. It may look like a typical Victorian suspension bridge, but was built as late as 1922 - in steel - by David Rowell & Company of Westminster. It is another of the many gifts to the town from the Shropshire Horticultural Society and a definite asset to the town's Quarry.

Kingsland Toll Bridge

The development of prosperous leafy suburban houses in Kingsland, largely connected with the removal of the School to the former Workhouse site, led to numerous schemes to replace the ferry.

Bridges over the Shropshire Severn

Atcham Bridge

Atcham

built - with style. The bridge carrying the main railway line from Shrewsbury to Wellington over the Severn close to Preston Boats was designed by William Baker, and opened in 1849. The line was jointly built by the Shrewsbury & Birmingham and Shropshire Union railway companies, and was capable of taking broad-gauge tracks if necessary. The bridge consists of two elegant cast-iron spans, each 101 foot long and made by the Coalbrookdale Company, springing from stone abutments and a central pier. During construction, two men fell off the bridge and drowned. The original ornate parapet was replaced by the present one when the bridge was given a much-needed face lift in the early 1980's.

Atcham Bridges

Atcham was another of the key medieval crossings of the Severn, though oddly was never guarded by a castle. The medieval bridge was built by Lilleshall Abbey, but between 1769 and 1771 a new stone bridge was built to the designs of John Gwynne. As in the case of his English Bridge in

Shrewsbury, this elegant seven-arch structure proved unsuitable to motor traffic and was replaced in the 1920's. Mercifully, it was not knocked down, and remains as one of the least altered examples of an eighteenth century main road bridge.

Immediately upstream is its reinforced concrete replacement, carrying what was, until recently, the ridiculously busy A5. Now it deals with the not inconsiderable local traffic. As a bridge it is not very attractive, and detracts from the older one alongside. It would, perhaps, have been better to case in the spandrels of the arches rather than expose the spindly nature of the construction used. It was designed by William Butler, county Surveyor, and built by the L G Mouchel partnership between 1927 and 1929. With a total length of over 450 feet, it is the longest of the county's Severn bridges.

The concrete bridge at Cressage

Telford's Buildwas Bridge showed a very sophisticated use of iron for its date

Cressage Bridge

The first Cressage Bridge was a timber toll-bridge built by Telford in the late-eighteenth century. It was replaced by the present bridge in 1913. From a distance, it looks as if it is made of stone. Only on closer inspection does its true character become clear - and particularly in the ornate balusters of the balustrade, many of which have rotted away to reveal the iron supports of the re-inforced concrete. In some ways, this can be seen as a forerunner of the later Atcham Bridge, and it was built by the same company; it is a shame that they did not copy it a little more closely.

Buildwas Bridge

There was a medieval bridge at Buildwas, largely repaired by Telford in the early

1790's but badly damaged in the Great Flood of 1795. It was decided to rebuild, and despite his background in masonry structures, Telford made the bold decision to use cast iron, improving on the original iron bridge downstream in the process. Movement of the banks led to that bridge being replaced in 1905 by another 'hog-backed Pratt truss' (like the Greyfriars foot bridge in Shrewsbury) and that in turn was replaced by the present bridge in 1992. It calls for little comment.

Ironbridge Power Station Bridges

There have been two power stations at the head of the Ironbridge Gorge, and both have been served by road bridges. Ironbridge 'A' opened in the 1930's and a girder bridge was built to connect it to the Ironbridge-Atcham road on the opposite bank. This still stands, but has been disused for many years. When the new Ironbridge 'B' station was under construction, a new concrete road bridge further downstream was started in 1964. Its busiest time came during the miners' strike of the mid-1980's when much of the power station's coal was temporarily transferred from rail to road, much to the inconvenience of the locals.

The Albert Edward Bridge, Ironbridge

Most of the coal to the power station still arrives by rail, and is carried from the main line near Madeley to the power station - which stands on part of the former Severn Valley line. The trains cross the river on a single span, 150 foot wide. It was, when it opened in 1864, claimed to be *'the largest cast-iron arch carrying a double line of railway that has yet been erected anywhere in the world'*. Designed by John Fowler, the ironwork was cast at Coalbrookdale. Although built for the quaintly named but seriously minded Much Wenlock, Craven Arms & Coalbrookdale Railway Company, it is virtually identical to the much-photographed Victoria Bridge at Arley on the preserved section of the Severn Valley Railway. That is a little longer, but only

The Albert Edward Bridge, once the longest of its type in the world, is still used

The most famous bridge over the river - the revolutionary Iron Bridge

took a single line of railway. The bridge was named after the future Edward the Seventh. It has survived only because of the coal traffic to the power station.

The Iron Bridge

The Iron Bridge is simply one of the most famous bridges in the world and much has been written about it. Suffice it to say that, before it was built, there were no bridges between Buildwas and Bridgnorth. This was a considerable problem in the Gorge area. In the 1770's plans were made to build a bridge, and it was the Shrewsbury architect Thomas Farnolls Pritchard who suggested one of iron, and produced some early designs for it. Although none of these were used, there seems little real doubt that Pritchard was largely responsible for the final design of the bridge, even though he died in 1777, the year work started. Any major changes were probably the work of Abraham Darby (the Third) and his own engineers. Darby put up much of the £5,000 it cost to build the bridge, and his company erected it.

Although not quite the first iron bridge in the world, it was the first major structure to use this material and its success revolutionised civil engineering the world over. It has come to be a symbol of the Industrial Revolution. The main castings are dated 1779 but the bridge was not officially opened until the first day of 1781, quickly becoming the major tourist attraction that it still is. Much of the techniques used in its construction belong to the world of the carpenter, with joints slotted and wedged together. Major changes have taken place to the approaches on either side, but the central arch has changed little over the past two centuries.

The dramatic new Jackfield Free Bridge approaching completion

In 1934 the bridge was closed to motor traffic and in 1950 became the property of Shropshire County Council. Unstable banks have caused problems for many years, and in the 1970's the bridge was the subject of a major restoration to its fabric and its footings.

The New Jackfield Free Bridge

The old Jackfield Free Bridge was a concrete structure funded by local subscription and opened in 1909. It was built, like Atcham and Cressage bridges, by L G Mouchell and partners. Officially it was the Haynes Memorial and Subscription Bridge. It was the 'free' bridge because no tolls were charged to cross - which was not the case on the Iron Bridge or Coalport bridge. By the 1980's it was beginning to cause concern and a replacement was decided on. Controversial plans to built this further upstream at Ladywood were scrapped. The new bridge has proven to be equally controversial. A single pylon stayed suspension bridge, it is certainly a robust and modern design. Although a little shocking now, perhaps it is what this innovative area deserves. Only time will tell. The bridge opened in 1994.

Coalport Bridge

Jackfield War Memorial Bridge

By no means the prettiest bridge on the river, this basic steel footbridge stands as one of the more useful memorials to those who lost their lives in the carnage of the First World War. It opened in 1922.

Coalport Bridge

Coalport Bridge is one of the most complex bridges over the river. It began as a simple enough timber bridge in 1777 of two spans. Badly damaged in the Great Flood of 1795, it was rebuilt as a composite single span structure with a timber deck on cast iron arches. Finally, in 1818, the timber deck was replaced by a cast iron one with cast iron parapets by John Onions. Unlike the Iron Bridge, it still carries motor traffic.

Apley Park, or Linley, Bridge

This graceful suspension bridge connected the wayside station of Linley, on the Severn

Apley Park Bridge

Valley line, with Apley Park on the opposite side of the river. It was built in 1909 by the same company that built the Port Hill footbridge in Shrewsbury, David Rowell & Company of Westminster. It is a private bridge and carries a private road, well off the beaten track.

Bridgnorth Bridge

Bridgnorth has one of the oldest bridge sites in the county. The very name 'Bridgnorth' is said to reflect that this was a settlement at a bridge to the north of the earlier one at Quatford - although that is unlikely. Quite how much is left of the later-medieval stone bridge is unclear, although the western span is possibly of fouteenth century date. Like many such bridges, it had carried a chapel -

Bridgnorth Bridge

in this case dedicated to the little known St. Osyth - and a gatehouse. The bridge suffered badly from floods. In the eighteenth century two arches were swept away on separate occasions and a third had to be replaced before it suffered the same fate. As a result, the bridge was largely rebuilt in 1813-14 by Thomas Simpson of Shrewsbury, and widened ten years later. Traditionally, the last working barge on the Shropshire Severn, carrying firebrick from the Gorge, ended its voyage by crashing into this bridge and sinking. The bridge was again widened and altered in 1960.

Bridgnorth By-Pass Bridge

Another example of the Department of Transport style, this steel and concrete bridge was built in the early 1980's. The bridge and its tall approaches destroy the once fine views from the High Town down the valley. Such is the price of progress.

Alveley Colliery Bridge, the last in the county

Alveley Colliery Bridge

At first glance the last bridge in the county seems to be little more than another 1960's-type concrete bridge, but then there seems also to be something missing - the road. But this is not some traffic planners mistake, a bridge built and never used. It was, in fact, a railway - and foot - bridge, and is older than it looks. It was built by the Highley Mining Company in 1936-7 to a design by the British Reinforced Concrete Engineering Company and took two narrow gauge tracks carrying colliery tubs. It linked the two collieries on opposite banks, Alveley and Highley. Its central span is 150 feet long, the two side spans 50 feet long. After the last colliery closed in 1969, the bridge was given by the National Coal Board to the County Council, and it now forms a useful pedestrian link between the country parks that have replaced the old mine sites.

The Shropshire Severn

Sunset at Atcham

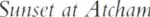

Sabrina

There is a gentle nymph not far from hence
That with moist curb sways the smooth Severn stream,
Sabrina is her name, a virgin pure...
Made goddess of the river: still she retains
Her maiden gentleness, and oft at eve
Visits the herds along the twilight meadows;
Helping all urchin blasts and ill-luck signs
That the shrewd meddling elf delights to make,
Which she with precious vialled liquors heals;
For which the shepherds at their festivals
Carol her goodness loud in rustic lays,
And throw sweet garland wreaths into her stream
Of pansies, pinks, and gaudy daffodils.

Sabrina Sings

By the rushy-fringed bank,
Where grows the willow and the osier dank,
    My sliding chariot stays,
Thick set with agate, and the azurn sheen
Of turkis blue, and emerald green,
    That in the channel strays:
Whilst from off the waters fleet
Thus I set my printless feet
O'er the cowslip's velvet head,
    That bends not as I tread.
Gentle swain, at thy request
    I am here!

Extracts from Comus by John Milton, first performed at Ludlow Castle in 1634

Flora and Fauna

Geology, climate and man have produced a rich and diverse collection of animals and plants in and along the banks of the Severn. John Tucker, Head of Conservation for the Shropshire Wildlife Trust, gives an insight into this splendid natural resource. It is a resource that needs to be cherished and protected - and it is perhaps a sad indictment of society that exact locations of some of the more endangered species cannot be given.

In ancient times the River Severn would have been the principal natural barrier between the lowlands of England to the east and the highlands of Wales to the west. Within Shropshire that ancient division still holds true. As the Severn first meanders slowly east and then south through the county, it separates high ground to its right bank from lower lands to its left. So by its passage from the Welsh hills to the English lowlands the River Severn is a living link between very different landscape and ecological types, sharing some of the wildlife of each. The Severn can also be a wild river, for heavy rains in its catchment in the hills often lead to flooding and consequent damage downstream. It is the diversity of its upper reaches, and those of it tributaries, together with its own structural diversity, which give the Severn its wildlife richness, conservation significance and charm.

The most obvious of all the flora in the valley are the trees. The alder, locally known as 'walla', is perhaps the most common waterside tree and our only cone-bearing deciduous species. Its seeds are much sought after by marauding winter flocks of siskins and less often redpolls, the former sometimes in groups of a hundred or more following river courses and their wallas. Alders are relatively fast-growing, especially from coppice stools. Coppicing a tree involves cutting all the stems down to just above the ground, usually in winter. The stool will begin to regrow in the following year. Pollarding is subtly different and is usually applied to willows. The majority of riverside alders are periodically coppiced to limit their threat to the banks as they mature and fall or get swept away;

The Severn in flood near the Isle

the Severn can be singularly malevolent when in spate. The wonderful richly orange-coloured wood, especially when newly cut, was used not so long ago for the soles of clogs and is still excellent for posts in wet ground, being very resistant to rot. Venice is built on alder piles.

A coppiced alder

Willows and watercourse so often go together, not least by the Severn. They are often pollarded. Pollarding a tree involves cutting the trunk at head height above which many branches will result. These will then grow from a swelling which will increase in size when the pollarding is repeated every few decades. The advantage of pollarding over coppicing is that the new growth occurs above the heads of cattle and horses which would otherwise eat it. Shropshire has a wide selection of willows, which have the habit of hybridising and causing baffling identification problems. We are fortunate in this county to have our own *Willows of Shropshire*, a key based on leaf size and shape written by a national willow expert from the county, Charles Sinker. Stopping to scrutinise the leaves of a peculiar willow is always a good excuse for a pause on the river bank on a long hot walk.

There are many fine specimen trees of a variety of species in Shropshire, some dating back many centuries. They have been studied in depth by Andrew Morton and he has written a very comprehensive and readable account of them. Some may be seen in short excursions from the river, often in the estates in the Severn Valley, for example at Attingham, Leighton and Loton Parks.

A pollarded willow

Where woodland comes close to the river there are chances to explore this habitat too. Excellent opportunities to penetrate deep into woodlands occur to the south of the county north of Bewdley where the Wyre Forest comes right down to the river. Wyre is owned largely by Forest Enterprise and English Nature who both

Flora and Fauna

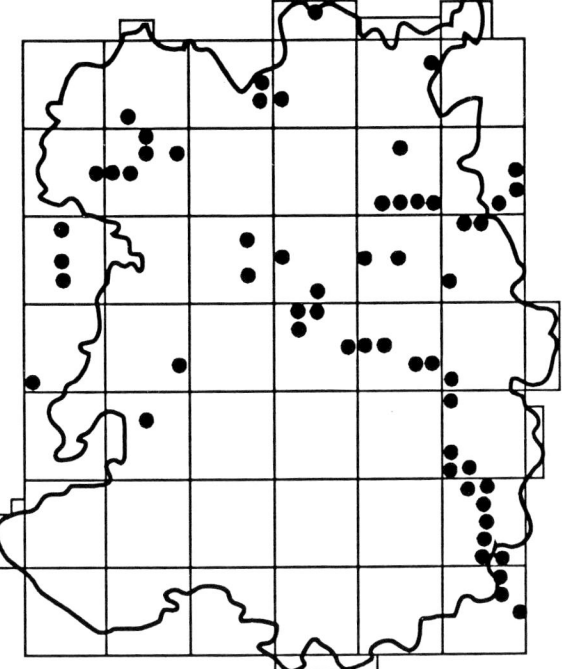

Flowering Rush distribution map. The lines of dots trace the course of the Severn and some of its tributaries

Flowering Rush

have open access policies and well developed woodland walk networks there. Further north the Severn Gorge Woodlands are reached easily by footpaths from Ironbridge, and are open to the public. Elsewhere do be careful not to trespass.

Flowering plants are also easy to find in spring and summer. Some waterside plants make their presence obvious, such as purple loosestrife announcing themselves with splashes of purple in upright spikes. Others take a little more searching out; the effort is well worthwhile and a fine example is the flowering rush. It is not a true rush though it shares the robust tubular structure of those ancient plants. It grows tall, at best up to head height, topped by a splendid star-burst of bright pink inflorescence itself up to a good hand-span across - a plant once seen never forgotten. The flowering rush is something of a Severn speciality, as the plant's distribution map shows, though it occurs also along some of the tributaries to the north, for example the Tern and the Perry.

Another spectacular plant of the Severn is the river water crowfoot which in places, in the height of summer, almost covers the river with its white and yellow flowers growing at the ends of long submerged stems reaching up through the waters of the shallower, stonier sections. The view of the river from the bridge in Bridgnorth is often spectacularly enhanced by blankets of this plant in July and August.

Among the other flowering plants to look out for especially along the Severn are the following; marsh and great yellow-cress, spear-leaved orache (below Shrewsbury), spiked water-milfoil, marsh woundwort, tansy on the banks, arrowhead, perfoliate pondweed, the all-too frequent alien Himalayan balsam and, not to forget the grasses, reed canary-grass. Of course plants as well as animals can move and may occur in odd places so if you see an unexpected or rare species do let the Shropshire Wildlife Trust know - they will pass the information to the Flora Project which maintains the county flora record.

A frequent riverside shrub is guelder rose. This is attractive throughout the spring and summer with distinctive three-lobed leaves followed by fine clusters of white flowers in summer developing into the waxy red fruits of autumn. While looking upwards at trees, watch out for mistletoe, but only in the south for it is a rare plant north of Bridgnorth.

Because of their size, shape, structure and texture, plants are also crucial to a wide range of animals, apart from their being the base of the food web. They offer for example anchorage and cover for fish eggs, haul-out points for emerging dragonflies, nest sites for moorhen at water level and reed warblers above it, and in a few places heronries atop trees within sight of the river and its flood-meadows.

Where the waters are not too deep, currents not too strong and where agriculture has not encroached to the very water's edge, then wild plants can take their chances and in the process offer opportunities for others. It is in the thicker, quieter and most secluded of such spots that the scattered individuals of the Severn's small otter population, which re-established itself from Wales in the 1980s, will lie up during the day. The vigilant observer, searching the mud under every bridge, might come across otter spoor but few ever see the animals themselves. An increasing toll of road casualties, alas, is one way in which we know about the county's increasing population.

As the otter has increased so, sadly, the water or bank vole has declined. The precise reasons are unclear but all the indications are that human activity is the root cause, including the possibility of competition with or predation by the now feral mink, which are frequently reported from Shropshire rivers. In any event 'Ratty' of *Wind in the Willows* is seldom seen on the Severn or its tributaries. A water vole survey by the Wildlife Trust in 1992 unearthed very few recent records but many lamentable accounts of disappearance and decline. All sightings should be reported to the Trust.

Just as the flowering rush is particularly common along the Severn, so also is the club-tailed dragonfly. In fact this magnificent animal is very much confined to the Severn, a national strong-

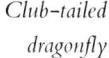
Club-tailed dragonfly

hold for the species, though there are occasional records from tributaries. They are best searched for from around mid-May to late June when adults are on the wing - a medium-sized dragonfly, the body coloured largely black and yellow. The diagnostic feature of the club-tailed is of course the distinctive tail-end from which the species derives its name - the rear fifth of the body broadens out making it look somewhat 'tail-heavy'. Further, if you get a good view, the club-tailed is unique among European dragonflies in having widely-spaced eyes (as have the damselflies) and the rear edge of the hind-wing is distinctive in having the appearance of a notch cut out where the wing attaches to the body.

Other dragonflies may be seen near the river, though few rely on it for breeding, preferring still or slow-flowing waters. Adults flying in twos in a peculiar tail-gripping-head formation are mating pairs while single animals repeatedly alighting on still water and dipping the tips of their tails in the water will be egg-laying females. Hunting dragonflies can be seen almost anywhere - they all actively seek prey and have the wide-spaced eyes and therefore the binocular vision necessary for the predatory life. In the flying stage of their life cycle dragonflies are free of the bond which keeps the larval stage in the mud for the rest of the year and they can spread to new waters. This is rather like the seed stage of wind dispersed plants.

Damselflies may also be seen. They are distinguished from dragonflies by their characteristic habit of folding their wings back over the body and the fact that their eyes are widely spaced, not touching as in dragonflies (with the single exception of the club-tailed). A damselfly to look out for is the banded agrion; in fact it will usually show itself off as the males display, flirting over floating vegetation, often in small groups and showing off four large deep blue patches, one towards the end of each wing, an animal well deserving its scientific name *Calopteryx splendens*. Other damselflies worth watching out for are the white-legged, for which the Severn is once again a national stronghold, the blue-tailed (the blue segment near the end of the body is diagnostic), the common blue and the unmistakeable large red.

The dramatic and delightful Kingfisher

There are innumerable other invertebrates associated with the river and its banks, variously food for birds, fish, or of course others of their kind. The identities and habits of most are of interest principally to the specialist, among whom I certainly do not number, and I will not attempt to elaborate further. The Wildlife Trust can always put

Flora and Fauna

A Sandmartin, captured in flight

you in touch with relevant experts if you are interested and would like to know more.

Birds are evident all along the Severn, especially in summer. In the woods, often near water, are the attractive and confiding pied flycatcher nesting in holes in old trees or in nest-boxes. Redstarts may also be found, especially by their song, but both species occur more frequently further south and west into the valleys of the hill country, well worth exploring on another day.

The first bird many people think of by the riverside is the kingfisher, though few see them. This is a great pity for they are one of our most brilliantly coloured birds and would not look out of place in the tropics. More people deserve to catch sight of one - here are some hints. As often as not they are seen only in flight, and seldom for long for they fly fast and as direct as a dart, frequently but not always low over the water. Above all listen out for the call, given in flight - a very distinctive, short and shrill "chee" or "chee-kee". So listen and watch out for a flash of blue over the water. You can afford to be a little selfish if you are with other people - if you do see one keep it in view and try to see where it lands. If you take your eyes off it you will certainly lose it yourself and in any case it will be gone before your companions can turn round. So keep it in view, watch for it to settle and then you can try to show your companions or have a better look yourself.

Other fish-eating birds are around and stealthy herons may be seen, especially in quiet reaches or on wet fields nearby. Don't be too surprised to see an occasional cormorant either - they do not breed inland but wander up and down the Severn on fishing trips. Another oddity you might come across is the mandarin duck, a rather gaudy escapee which occasionally breeds on the river not far south of Bridgnorth.

Sand martins nest in small colonies by the Severn, in secure sites where the vertical banks drop straight into the water and afford security for their broods at the end of their self-excavated tunnels into the earth or sand. Sadly the Shropshire population is still much reduced, mirroring the national

A Dipper

decline since the 1960s. Grey wagtails (resident) occur along the Severn, though they prefer the smaller and faster streams, while their close relative the yellow wagtail (a summer visitor) may be found breeding in wet fields close to the river, especially above Shrewsbury. Dippers show the opposite trend - they occasionally breed by the Severn, but more frequently on its tributaries, especially south-west of Shrewsbury. They can be as elusive as kingfishers and the hints for finding them apply almost equally here - except of course that the birds are black and white. Anyone planning birding along the river, or indeed anywhere else in the county, would be wise to consult in advance the Shropshire Ornithological Society's *An Atlas of the Breeding Birds of Shropshire* for maps and accounts of the birds which may be found on any particular trip.

Wildlife is a precious resource and depends on complex infrastructures and relationships to survive. Alterations to these can endanger the environment. The plans to create an artificial navigation on the Severn by creating weirs and locks, and introducing more powered craft will do just that. Suffice it to say that every organisation in the region involved in environmental issues, including the Wildlife Trust, the Shropshire Ornithological Society, canoeing groups and fishing clubs, have declared themselves against these proposals.

The corridor of the river Severn offers a wonderful introductory route through the heart of Shropshire. Exploring its moods, its bordering habitats and wildlife and the towns, villages and hostelries along its length, brings tantalising views of Shropshire's other attractions. Yet to be discovered may be the depths of the Wyre Forest, the lanes of Bridgnorth upper town, the heights of the Wrekin, the views of Shrewsbury from Haughmond Hill, the wide expanses of the south Shropshire hills and the views of Wales, and the upper Severn's meanders from Rodney's Pillar atop the Breidden.

MANAGING THE RIVER

The official guardian of the Severn is the recently formed National Rivers Authority. Its job, since 1989, is to regulate the quantity and quality of the water taken from the river and to guard against floods. Wayne Baker, the NRA's Regional Public Relations Manager, explains:

The Severn-Trent Region of the National Rivers Authority covers an area of more than eight thousand square miles and has more than four thousand miles of river to look after. It is the second largest of the eight regions and is basically sub-divided into the Severn and Trent catchment areas. The catchment area of the Severn covers nearly four and a half thousand square miles, and the NRA offices for the Upper Severn are based in Shrewsbury.

The river has always been a very important source of water, and this century has seen demand steadily increasing. To meet this need there are three main intakes from the river. Shrewsbury Corporation completed their Shelton waterworks just upstream of the town in 1935, and this now provides more than thirty thousand million litres of water every day for the town and the area around it.

A much larger intake at Hampton Loade, downstream of Bridgnorth, provides about six times this amount for use in the Black Country and Wolverhampton areas. Many parts of south Shropshire are supplied by the third, and much smaller, intake at Trimpley, just over the county boundary in Worcestershire. Small reservoirs have also been built at Trimpley and at Chelmarsh to maintain supplies to these areas in the rare event of accidental pollution of the river.

As the demands on the river increase, it has become necessary to regulate the amount of water being taken from it. This ensures that enough flows on to be used further downstream, and that

Winter floods at Atcham

there is always enough in the county itself. The NRA controls the amount of water taken through a system of abstraction licences. It also controls the reservoirs in the Welsh head-waters of the Severn to make sure that the proper flows are maintained throughout the dry summer months when water demand is high.

During the past ten years an additional supply of water has been developed by the NRA in Shropshire to increase the levels of the summer flows. Known as the Shropshire Groundwater Project, when completed it will provide up to an extra 225 million litres of water a day to top up the river. In this way the amount of water taken from the river can be steadily increased without sacrificing the levels of the river itself - so essential for the water quality, the fisheries, and other amenity uses.

The quality of water is obviously a key concern of the NRA. Regular samples are taken from a number of sites on the Severn and its tributaries to check it. These ensure that its quality is not declining and detect any pollution invisible to the naked eye. Throughout the Severn-Trent region there are over a thousand monitoring sites. All discharges into the river are also regularly checked. If they do not meet the conditions laid down in their licences, the NRA can prosecute those responsible.

Water sampling

The most widely used means of checking the water quality is biological monitoring. It is a means of obtaining faunal records and estimates of the biological quality of the watercourses. The benefits of biological monitoring have been recognised since the start of the century. Development of the sampling process has resulted in nationally used score systems - and the methods used play a central role in pollution control throughout the United Kingdom.

Chemical analysis of water samples normally provides only spot records or checks. This type of sampling, and therefore the information gained from it, is mostly limited to weekdays and daylight hours - so adverse conditions can be missed. On the other hand, biological monitoring provides information over a longer period of time. It can assess the impact of the water chemistry on the natural bed-living fauna. Any pollutant in the water will create an imbalance in that community and one group of organisms may be reduced or even eliminated.

The method of biological sampling used depends on the site. Those on rivers are usually samples from within the river itself and taken across its full width. Material is captured in a sample net held immediately downstream of the operator for three minutes. The collected samples are examined as soon as possible back at the laboratory, and the data is summarised as a biological score.

In general, most sites on the Welsh section of the Severn are of consistently good quality, despite some recent acidification in the uppermost reaches. The good quality of the river, and its tributaries, is maintained throughout Shropshire, despite organic enrichment from the major conurbations of Shrewsbury and Telford. Even further downstream, below the confluence of the fairly polluted Stour, it is still classed as being of good quality.

The water in the Severn also has to be controlled. It is subject to flooding, and sometimes floods can see the water level rise by more than four metres. This is by no means a recent phenomenon - and is a natural one. As the agency responsible for tackling the flooding issue, the NRA have taken firm steps to combat the problem.

Amongst the earliest attempts at flood alleviation are the embankments constructed in the area around Melverley and further upstream. These argaes takes their name from the Welsh word for a wall or embankment and were mostly built towards the end of the eighteenth century under the Enclosure Acts of that time. Over the years these embankments have been affected by both the movement of the river and by the actions of rabbits and moles burrowing into them. They were also built rather cheaply, using the minimum amount of earth and often with steep sides making them difficult to maintain. Their repair is the responsibility of the NRA and now the argaes are being improved, strengthened and made easier to maintain. The same degree of protection is being retained and levels are not being altered at all.

At the end of 1993, the long-awaited plans for a four million pound flood alleviation scheme for Shrewsbury were announced. This is aimed to protect up to four hundred properties and will hopefully reduce the possibility of flooding from once every decade to once every century. The plans have been drawn up after extensive studies and investigations by NRA designers and engineers of several different options - and after a great deal of public consultation. Much of the work will simply involve strengthening and raising existing defences. New work is to be blended in with existing features, using, for example, re-used brick or stone to face concrete or steel piling. At present the scheme is still being considered by the local authority and other relevant bodies.

The river near the Gay Meadow, Shrewsbury

The NRA also liaises and advises all the county's local planning authorities to prevent any new developments that might be subject to flooding - or that might increase the likelihood of flooding for existing properties.

Another important aspect of the authority's work is its flood warning system that covers the whole of the Severn, the Trent, and their tributaries. Sophisticated state-of-the-art computerised monitoring equipment at the flow forecasting centre in the NRA regional headquarters at Solihull, complemented by teams at Shrewsbury and Tewkesbury, provide round-the-clock data on river levels.

Using weather forecasts and radar information on expected rainfall patterns, the flow forecasting team is able to produce computer models to give an up-to-date picture of what will happen at given stretches of the river during the following forty-eight hours. This then enables the NRA, if necessary, to issue flood warnings to the police who then inform the public. The NRA's emergency workforce ensures that the flood control defences are working properly and that bridges are cleared of floating debris.

Finally, the NRA is also actively involved in fisheries and conservation. The Severn is a top quality river supporting almost every type of freshwater fish - although fishing on the river was affected in the nineteenth century by the building of weirs on the section below Worcester. Rudimentary fish passes were built at many of the weirs - and, indeed, there is such a pass at the flood-prevention weir at Shrewsbury. Surveys of fish stock are carried out regularly by fisheries staff based at the area office in Shrewsbury. Fish have also been transferred from the upper Severn for restocking in other parts of the Severn-Trent region. The NRA offers free coarse fishing at its own fisheries along the upper reaches of the river.

Conservation schemes are an important part of the day-to-day work of the NRA. Numerous schemes involving the public and school-children have been developed in Shropshire. These include an otter project that monitors the spread and encourages the return of this shy creature by providing suitable habitats as part of flood prevention and conservation schemes. Further details of the NRA and its work are available from the Public Relations section.

A coxed four on the river by Shrewsbury's Quarry Park

RECREATION

The Shropshire Severn is a great recreational resource, though one not really that well used. It has always been famous for its fishing, and in season the banks can get quite crowded with practitioners of this inscrutable activity. The National Rivers Authority issue licences and there are several different angling clubs that own or rent parts of the banks.

Most people will get their relaxation from simply strolling along relatively short stretches of the river bank, and many will just drive to a suitable spot and not venture too far from their cars or buses. There are such places along the river, but for the more adventurous their are better ways of getting the most from it.

Walking

The Shropshire Severn is, for the most part, shunned by roads and by traffic. The pleasant, and sometimes spectacular landscape, through which it flows offers fine, and not too challenging, walking. Following the river itself in the upper reaches, however, can be a frustrating experience. Somehow, incomprehensibly, the age old right of way along its tow paths has been extinguished in many places. To make matters worse, the many ferries still optimistically being marked on maps earlier this century have all but gone; only that at Hampton Load remains. In the old days some were vital links in traditional footpaths, and others enabled the tow horses to cross the river when the prescribed tow-path swopped banks.

The end of the river trade and the rise of the motor car has made the river ferry long obsolete. Losing the rights to the tow paths was bad enough. Far more recently, a much sillier loss to the

Recreational canoeists at Coalport

public was the failure of British Railways and the local authorities to agree to develop the track bed of the Severn Valley line as a cycle way and footpath after the line closed in 1963. It would have been a tremendous asset to tourism in this county - but as was the case elsewhere, the opportunity was spurned.

Nowadays, anyone wishing to follow the course of the Severn has to accept the occasional diversion away from it, or some back-tracking. A good Ordnance survey map, preferably one of the 1:25000 type, and a stout pair of boots are all the specialist equipment needed for walking.

It is possible with the aid of such maps to plan a few circular routes in the region upstream of Shrewsbury, but there are few opportunities to follow the river itself for any great distances. The first walk of any length along the bank is from the end of Underdale Road, which follows the river all the way round through to the old A5 near Atcham - a once splendid walk now a little marred in parts by the by-pass. The next is not until the Ironbridge Gorge.

It is possible to follow the river all the way through the Gorge on the north bank - and to continue for several miles past Coalport. Annoyingly, it would be possible to carry on all the way to Worcestershire - but the path crosses the river at the site of the Sutton Maddock fish weir! Swimming in the river is most definitely not recommended, no matter how low or inviting the water looks. At Sutton Maddock, incidentally, the nearby sewerage works makes such activity unlikely to appeal, though the walk as far as the weir is still worth the back-tracking to Coalport. To get to that tantalising opposite bank and its footpath means more walking, this time from footpaths leading to the river off the Broseley to Bridgnorth road. Past Bridgnorth, arranging walks of varying lengths is easy and footpaths follow the bank all the way. There can be few better ways of recovering from such exercise than by sitting in an antique Severn Valley Railway carriage being hauled by a steam locomotive back up to where you started.

Notes on Wheelchair Access

Perhaps not surprisingly to most disabled people, wheelchair access to the river is generally poor. In the country this is predictable, but in the towns and villages, disappointing. There are toilet

An earlier generation enjoying the river bank - a sketch by Edward Pryce Owen of 1834

facilities for disabled people at the new Picnic Site off the A5 at Montford Bridge, but no one seems to have thought to provide even a simple disabled access to the nearby riverside.

In Shrewsbury, it is possible to follow the river round most of the way on the inside of the loop. Perhaps the best place to park for the independent traveller is in the Greyfriars Car Park just off Wyle Cop. From there the tarmacadamed road by the river is easily accessible. It is possible to follow the river downstream as far as the weir - though the cobbles under the railway bridge are difficult to negotiate and the only real bit of interest is the view of the English Bridge. Upstream, the avenue of limes goes around the lovely Quarry park, where there are toilet facilities at the Porthill Suspension bridge. In general, access around the town is poor because of the terrain.

Downstream, there are only one or two isolated places that have good access, but several good viewpoints from a parked car. More really should be done in the Ironbridge gorge area. The Museum tries its best, but it is the area on the Wharfage that needs to be improved. The pavement are too narrow and too uneven for comfortable wheelchair travel. The best area for access is picturesque Dale End Park, and there are facilities at the main car park by the Museum of the River.

Bridgnorth is another town whose terrain makes live for the disabled difficult. The walks around the castle are quite flat and well paved, and there are good views. The rest of the town is a little difficult to get round. The Severn Valley Railway will always try and help its disabled passengers. There are toilet facilities at Bridgnorth and Kidderminster stations. There are more facilities at both country park sites at Highley and Alveley, but access to the banks is limited by the steepness of the terrain.

On the Water

It is on the water itself that a great deal of fun could be had, and the river can be seen from a very different perspective. For the keen and sporty, there are rowing clubs at Shrewsbury, Ironbridge and Bridgnorth, and canoe clubs at Shrewsbury and Telford. For

A determined slalom competitor on Jackfield rapid

This houseboat and its swimmers are thought to have been moored somewhere on the Shropshire Severn, but where?

the less active, row-boats and canoes can be hired in Shrewsbury, and boat trips are provided in the county town and also at Ironbridge. One company offers a variety of trips in canoes, including one linked in with the Severn Valley Railway. The more adventurous can organise their own trips.

The Severn is a rarity amongst English rivers. The law of England and Wales regarding rivers is far more reactionary than that on the Continent, or even in Scotland. There, the rivers are seen as rights of way that can be used by anyone provided they abide by the law. In England and Wales, there is usually no such right of way; the river is owned completely by those who own the banks, and only they can say if passage will be granted. Thus most of England's rivers are effectively out of bounds to canoeists and boaters. The Severn, though, because of its historic status as the 'King's High Stream of Severn', is a free river - free of such restrictions and open to all. It is thus possible to paddle or row all the way from Melverley to the sea. Navigating the Shropshire Severn can be an interesting way of spending a few days away from it all and getting a closer look at nature.

It is not a particularly dangerous river, though all rivers have to be treated with caution even in the summer months. Undertows and unexpected deep troughs can catch out the unwary, often with fatal results. Apart from the risk of grounding in low water, and of being swept away in the currents at times of spate, there are no really dangerous sections of river. The weir at Shrewsbury should be avoided by row-boats and by inexperienced canoeists, and the rapids at Jackfield, just below the Free Bridge, where ranking canoe slalom events are held regularly, need to be treated with respect. If in doubt, don't!

There are a few obvious safety rules to follow, especially if your trip takes you away from the frequented parts of the river. Always wear a buoyancy aid or life-jacket, and always let people know where you are and how long you expect to be. Above all, never swim in the river unless you have to.

There are other things to bear in mind as well. Watch out for anglers and don't get entangled in their lines. Remember, you have a right to be on the water, but they have their right to their enjoyment too. Finally, whilst the river is a right of way, be sure that you do not trespass on the banks getting to and from the water or during the trip.

Suggested Reading

The Natural River

Deans, P, Sankey, J, Tucker, J, Whittles, D and Wright, C, AN ATLAS OF THE BREEDING BIRDS OF SHROPSHIRE (1992)

Morton, A, THE TREES OF SHROPSHIRE (1986)

Riley, AM, A NATURAL HISTORY OF THE BUTTERFLIES AND MOTHS OF SHROPSHIRE (1981)

Sinker, CA, Packham, JR, Trueman, IC, Oswald, PH, Perring, FH & Prestwood, WV, ECOLOGICAL FLORA OF THE SHROPSHIRE REGION (1985)

Toghill, P, GEOLOGY IN SHROPSHIRE (1990)

Man and the River

Blackwall, A, HISTORIC BRIDGES OF SHROPSHIRE (1985)

Clark, C, THE ENGLISH HERITAGE BOOK OF THE IRONBRIDGE GORGE (1993)

Marshall, J, THE SEVERN VALLEY RAILWAY (1989)

Morriss, RK, THE BUILDINGS OF SHREWSBURY (1993)

Morriss, RK, CANALS OF SHROPSHIRE (1191)

Trinder, B, THE INDUSTRIAL REVOLUTION IN SHROPSHIRE (1981)

Kissack, K, THE RIVER SEVERN (1987)

More books on Shropshire published by Shropshire Books

SHROPSHIRE SEASONS Gordon Dickins £14.99

SHROPSHIRE FROM THE AIR Michael Watson & Chris Musson £13.99

CHURCHES OF SHROPSHIRE Lawrence Garner £8.99

SHROPSHIRE MERES & MOSSES Nigel Jones £4.99

For a complete list of Shropshire Books, please contact:

Shropshire Books
Shropshire Leisure Services
Winston Churchill Building
Radbrook Centre
SHREWSBURY SY3 9BJ
Shropshire